# FORGOTTEN
## MARYLAND
## COCKTAILS

# FORGOTTEN
## MARYLAND
## COCKTAILS

### A HISTORY OF DRINKING IN THE FREE STATE

GREGORY PRIEBE & NICOLE PRIEBE

*Foreword by Aaron Joseph*

AMERICAN PALATE

Published by American Palate
A Division of The History Press
Charleston, SC 29403
www.historypress.net

First published 2015

Manufactured in the United States

ISBN 978.1.62619.856.2

Library of Congress Control Number: 2015934345

*To our parents, for giving us our first drinks and our first reasons to drink.*
*Love always, Greg and Nicole*

# CONTENTS

# CONTENTS

# FOREWORD

*There is a difference between cocktails and drinks.*
*Of the two, what do you prefer to make?*

This question was posed to me when I first entered the craft of bartending. At the time I didn't have the slightest idea that there was a difference. To me, a cocktail could be anything from a rum and Coke to an Alabama Slammer, and as long as it had some type of spirit and maybe a mixer it was a cocktail. Fast-forward thirteen years: I look back on those days and cringe at the ignorance that I displayed, and I wonder if anyone else shared this same mentality. My mentor at the time simply replied, "Cocktails have history, they have class. They are well thought out recipes to achieve a balance and have a direction. To understand the difference, you must understand the definition of a cocktail and the history behind them."

As a bartender in Baltimore, I have always been inquisitive about the history of drinking in this town. As I did some research, I realized that Charm City was more than just your average beer and vodka town. Places like the Lord of Baltimore Hotel, the Owl Bar and Elkridge Country Club were the prominent establishments where cocktails and spirits flowed abundantly. Also, spirits, like rye whisky and rum, were once associated with Maryland as often as crabs and Old Bay are mentioned today. This town had class and direction when it came to cocktails and has great history when it comes to a vibrant cocktail scene. But where did it all go? Why did it disappear? These were questions that I often asked members of our community, and often they were answered with inconclusive results. It wasn't until I went to a cocktail conference in New Orleans—Tales of the Cocktail—that I began to get traction on my pursuit for answers. It was there that I met up with a wonderful cocktail enthusiast, Greg Priebe, and he helped to enlighten me with the rich history of Baltimore's cocktail scene. It was there sitting in an old bar in New Orleans that I learned that Baltimore had a huge part of an epic era in cocktails.

Charm City, a place that is known for its small-town feel, blue-collar workforce and rough exterior, is now moving back to that forgotten and polished era that once was lost over time. Cocktails like the Orange Crush or the Black-Eyed Susan are still recognized as popular libations in this town but are rivaled by classics like the Preakness Cocktail and the Baltimore Southside. With an emphasis on quality and creativity when it comes to cocktails, we as bartenders are now seeing an influx of demand for classic styles like egg white sours, shrubs and punches. There is a cocktail movement happening! Cocktails are not just made with pre-mixed sours and canned juice. They are being created like pieces of art. Every little aspect of creating cocktails now has a focus on quality, seasonality and balance. There are now culinary-influenced cocktails, spirit-driven classics and, of course, the "dealer's choice" that now make up the cocktail scene here in Baltimore. As bartenders and cocktail ambassadors in this community, we have committed to providing our guests with the best and most innovative creations that not only incorporate local produce but also highlight quality spirits to give our consumers the best possible product available. Who would have thought that going to the farmers' market under the JFX would be a part of a regular routine to create the cocktail of the week? Passion for the craft has now taken over the city, and from the direction I am seeing, it's likely here to stay.

As we continue with this progression of cocktails in Baltimore, I can't help but reflect on the history that once made this state a prominent place to imbibe. As a bartender, a book like this is not only a blessing but also an invaluable resource. It takes a passionate and dedicated person to write a book like this, and I love that Greg and Nicole have taken the time to record the history and feature the trends that are now a relative part of our cocktail scene. It was a long conversation with a good friend that helped answer the questions that I had about drinking in Maryland. Hopefully this book will answer those same questions and maybe evoke more questions that will make drinking in Maryland as prideful as the community that embraces it.

Happy drinking!

**AARON JOSEPH**
*Head Bartender*
*Wit & Wisdom*

# ACKNOWLEDGEMENTS

T his book has been one crazy ride, and we would like to give out our deepest thanks to everyone who made it all possible:

First off, we would like to thank the great Maryland mixologists whom we have come to know over the past few years. Aaron Joseph, Brendan Dorr, Doug Atwell, Jeff Levy and Melissa Ray and Perez Klebahn, thank you all for elevating the Baltimore cocktail scene. Without your insight and willingness to resurrect some of the cocktails printed here, this whole project would have been much more difficult and a whole heck of a lot less fun. Thanks also for letting us print your fantastic original creations; they are certainly cocktails that should not be forgotten!

To Maryland craft distilleries and even to those out of state who have endeavored to resurrect the true spirit of Maryland rye—Ben Lyon and Jaime Windon, of Lyon Distilling; Andy Keller, of Blackwater & Sloop Betty; Ned White, of New England Distilling; and Leopold Distilling—our hats are off to all of you.

Of the many friends we see each year at Tales of the Cocktail in New Orleans, we'd like to single out Addie K. Martin for hooking us up with her contacts at The History Press and our amazingly talented friend Warren "The Cocktail Whisperer" Bobrow for inspiring us with his passion for all things spirit and cocktail related and proving to us—once and for all—that yes, you can reinvent yourself if you truly have the will and the courage to do so.

# ACKNOWLEDGEMENTS

Thank you to our families, for all of the encouragement and support throughout this project and for agreeing to be our guinea pigs when we showed up on your doorstep with yet another arcane alcoholic creation.

Last, but most certainly not least, to the A History of Drinking Team, both official and un-: Keith and Jessica Hawks for being our early cheerleaders and handling our "proof of concept" photo shoots; Richard Smith, Doug Wood and Adam Fantom—thank you for the road trips and endless pub and bar crawls; Melissa Harris, for finding all the super-cool vintage barware shown throughout the book; and Keith and Christina Hipsley, thanks, well, for everything.

# INTRODUCTION

*No tour of Baltimore is complete, without driving past something that used to be there.*
*—Laura Lippman, crime novelist and former* Baltimore Sun *writer*

Drinking in Maryland is about a lot more than "Kosher Bohs" and hubcap margaritas. For the uninitiated in local lore and many a dive bar drink offerings, the "Kosher Boh" is a National Bohemian Beer, aka Natty Boh, with a shot of Pikesville Rye. Neither is produced in Maryland anymore, but there are still a few diehard fans out there who believe in the authenticity of the "Kosher Boh" as a local drink. Maryland, in fact, has lot more to offer.

What we hold in our glasses today has been, for a large part, determined by what was available in the state over the course of its more than three hundred years of history. Many of the recipes in this book will demonstrate how Marylanders made use of what they had to get the libations they wanted. Of course, there was a lot that couldn't be grown in Maryland or crops that couldn't be spared for fermenting, and a lot of our "make do" measures are showcased in early recipes for entertaining. Later on in the book, we will take you through Maryland's early distilling years and the introduction of its own style of rye whiskey.

Maryland households and hospitality establishments developed signature recipes for local favorites, like the apple toddy or eggnog. As time passed and tastes changed, our once grand hotels ushered in the age of the cocktail.

Of course, Prohibition tried to put a stop to all the fun, but Maryland didn't take this lying down. A number of prominent politicians rejected Prohibition and fought it by filing repeal efforts or through simple nonenforcement. Some, risking prison time, resorted to home fermentation in defiance of this assault on states' rights. Maryland also had H.L. Mencken leading the charge against the law with his relentless wit.

After the repeal, it took a long time for Maryland to begin distilling again, but bartenders started creating new cocktails immediately, like the still famous Baltimore Southside and Preakness cocktails. Upon the arrival of the vodka age, there was a dark turn in local cocktails when favorites were of the tall and sweet variety, seemingly designed so that whatever lady you purchased one (of three) for would not remember your name the next day. Fortunately, that is all changing.

Now, Maryland has begun distilling spirits again, and those spirits are being put to good use by local bartenders, who have contributed their favorite recipes to this book and some modern twists to old classics. As you read this book, you will find out more about the history of Maryland and how that shaped our drinking habits. Or maybe you'll find out what was happening that made us need a drink. Feel free to drink along with us by making use of the many recipes included throughout this book.

# TOOLS OF THE TRADE

## SHAKERS

There are three major styles of shakers to choose from, each with its own merits and disadvantages. It may take some time and practice before you decide which style suits you best.

COBBLER SHAKER: The standard, three-piece shaker included with most basic home-bartender starter sets. It consists of a metal shaker tin; a top section with a small, integral strainer; and a metal cap. This model is good for beginners but is prone to ice jamming up the strainer if used multiple times in an evening.

BOSTON SHAKER: The choice of professionals and more advanced home mixologists, this is a two-part shaker consisting of a pint-style glass and a metal mixing tin. Getting the right "magic seal" does require practice, as does separating the two halves once a drink has been shaken. This style also requires the use of a separate strainer. Boston shakers composed of two metal tins are now in fashion at many higher-end craft cocktail bars.

PARISIAN SHAKER: The middle ground between the two styles and our personal favorite. This model is similar to the cobbler shaker, with a metal mixing tin topped with a metal cap, but forgoes the strainer, making it less prone to being jammed up by ice but requiring the use of another strainer. It is easier to separate after shaking than the Boston shaker.

## MIXING GLASSES

While there is absolutely no reason why cocktails can't be stirred in a pint glass or the mixing tin of the shaker, we have taken a liking to the Japanese-style spouted mixing glasses that are on the market today. Ranging between thirty and forty dollars, they are a mid-level investment of the home cocktail enthusiast but give the added comfort of having a dedicated tool for this specific task.

## STRAINERS

Once you progress beyond the three-piece shaker, investing in both types of cocktail strainers will be a logical next step. While one can usually perform double-duty, they were designed originally to fit one specific half of the shaker.

HAWTHORNE STRAINER: This is the model that will be the most familiar to the beginning home bartender. Multi-pronged with an embedded spring, the Hawthorne strainer is designed to fit the metal tin side of the Boston shaker and is designed to keep the spent ice from dropping into the finished shaken cocktail.

JULEP STRAINER: Resembling a stumpy, fat-headed slotted spoon on steroids, this strainer is now mated with the pint glass end of the shaker and keeps unwanted ice and other large particles from falling into the cocktail glass. Originally, this strainer was designed to keep ice from hitting the poorly maintained teeth of julep drinkers prior to improvements in dentistry.

## OTHER TOOLS ESSENTIAL TO THE MARYLAND MIXOLOGIST'S CRAFT

BAR SPOON: A long handled—sometimes twisted—metal spoon used for stirring cocktails. Most basic bar sets will include a cheap one with the obligatory red plastic tip, which is fine for a start, but throw it away (or stick it in your traveling bar kit) when you have upgraded to a proper one. Sturdier versions can be purchased in the fifteen- to thirty-dollar range and may even come with a basic muddler or garnish fork opposite the spoon end. To re-create the old-school country club–era bartender, you may want to peruse eBay for the traditional long-handled engraved silver Kirk Steiff iced tea spoon. This may put you back fifty dollars or more for a single spoon, but you will look good stirring up a pitcher of authentic Baltimore Southsides for your summer garden parties.

MUDDLER: A small wooden (traditionally) club-like tool used to gently mash herbs, sugar cubes or other items in the bottom of a mixing glass. You should try to find one that fits your hand comfortably. The mashing end comes in both smooth and jagged.

LEMON/LIME JUICER: Sometimes referred to as the "Mexican elbow," these hand-held juicers can be found in yellow and green—depending on lemon or lime—varieties in most grocery and kitchen supply stores.

VEGETABLE PEELER: An essential tool for removing citrus peels for garnishes. It may take a bit of practice before you can accurately separate the peel and leave behind the bitter white pith on the fruit itself.

JIGGERS: Accurate measurement is the key to great cocktails. Sure, you can be the free-pour flair mixologist all you want, but sometimes even a quarter ounce too much can throw off the balance of a drink and make it unpalatable. Jiggers come in almost every measure, and you can take your pick of metal or plastic. At a bare minimum, have on hand jiggers in the denominations of half an ounce, three-quarters of an ounce, one ounce and two ounces. If you are just starting out and don't want to go fumbling through to find what you need, OXO makes a line of mini plastic measuring cups that have most of the required measures.

CORKSCREW: Always good to have on hand while working with wine. You can go the fully automatic route for a stress-free experience, but mastering the waiter's corkscrew multi-tool is a rite of passage any aspiring bartender should go through.

BOTTLE OPENER: You'll need one of these to pop the caps off craft beers and higher-end sodas. Opt for a key-ring version for Eagle Scout–style preparedness and be the savior of the party.

PARING KNIFE: Keep one of these aside for dedicated garnish duty.

CUTTING BOARD: Again, this will come in handy when you find yourself cutting garnishes for all these classic drinks.

### Advanced Tools

File these under the "nice to have" heading. Generally you can get away without them, but here are a few tools to make certain tasks easier.

CHANNEL KNIFE: This specialized knife is perfect for creating those ultra-thin citrus peel spirals popular during the early days of the American cocktail renaissance.

ICE CRUSHER: For producing the vast amount of crushed "snowball ice" needed for your Maryland Mint Juleps or Frozen Ryes, you can always hunt down a vintage countertop electric or manual ice crusher from your local thrift store or charity shop. If you want to build up your arm muscles and relieve built-up tension, you can always order one of the Lewis bag-and-mallet combinations from an online bar supply store.

# GLASSWARE

If you are limiting yourself to the drinks contained within this book, you will be able to get away with a minimum array of glass types, but the essentials are:

COCKTAIL: Also referred to as the "martini glass," this stemmed, usually v-shaped glass can be used to serve up everything from the Belvedere to the Preakness and many more in between.

ROCKS: This glass is sometimes referred to as the lowball, but they're essentially the same thing. All of your old-fashioned cocktails can be served with a modicum of ice in this glass, which is generally around eight ounces in capacity.

COLLINS: This ten- to twelve-ounce glass is par for the course for the country club–style Frozen Rye. It is sometimes synonymous with the slightly smaller highball glass, which only holds between eight and ten ounces.

PUNCH: A good deal of the drinks in the book are in punch form, and if you are preparing the whole recipe, you'll also need the hardware. If you weren't lucky enough to have been left one as an inheritance, you can easily secure one at your local thrift store. All of this paraphernalia might give you storage issues, but drinks served in this manner will save you from being chained to the bar throughout your entire party.

# THE WELL-STOCKED MARYLAND BAR

## WHISK(E)Y

RYE WHISKEY: Maryland rye is making a comeback, and two Eastern Shore distilleries have rolled out their renditions of white rye and should have aged examples ready sometime in 2015. In the meantime, there are also several out-of-state operations producing "Maryland-style Rye." If you attempt to make the rye-based cocktails in this book, resist the urge to go with the modern high-rye content spirits (Maryland rye was typically only 51 to 55 percent rye) such as the ones sourced out of Midwest Grain Products under various "craft" labels, as they will simply overpower the rest of the ingredients. When in doubt, you can always fall back on Pikesville; the taste won't suffer, and your wallet will thank you.

SCOTCH: Don't worry, we won't be venturing into single-malt territory here. Any recipe calling for Scotch whisky in this book is easily handled with a nice blended one.

IRISH WHISKEY: Seriously, don't break the bank on this one, as there's no need to break out the Redbreast your dad has secreted away for next St. Patrick's day. Any mid-shelf variety will do here.

# RUM

This is where things get a wee bit complicated. Rum is a sugar distillate, sometimes from cane juice, sometimes from sugar, but most commonly from molasses. For drinks prior to Prohibition, you are going to want to go with the "pirate juice"–style rums. Pot-still creations are your friends here, and you will want the funky, full of estery-goodness style that used to be common to the English-controlled Caribbean. For drinks developed from the 1960s onward, Baltimore—and especially the sailing community—has always had a special affinity for Mount Gay and Meyers rums. If you want to buy local, both Lyon and Blackwater Distilling have produced great rums.

# VODKA

If you are just re-creating Black-Eyed Susans (shame on you) or Orange Crushes at home, there is no need at all to go full-premium here. Any mid-shelf brand will do. For local offerings, check out Blackwater Distilling's Sloop Betty and Fiore's Blue Crab Vodka—don't worry, it's just the name; it doesn't actually taste like crab.

# BRANDY

BRANDY/COGNAC: This one is pretty straightforward. Brandy is an aged spirit distilled from grapes. For recipes calling for brandy, you can cough up a bit of cash for the French stuff or get away with using the lower price point domestic brandy (don't go too cheap though); either should do fine. Cognac is brandy that comes out of the Cognac region of France, so you are pretty much stuck there, but you can stick to VS rather than VSOP since you will be mixing and not drinking it straight. We've always been quite partial to CAMUS.

APPLE BRANDY: We recommend either Laird's Bottled in Bond Apple Brandy or its Old Aged Apple Brandy. Steer clear of the Applejack iteration since it is cut with neutral grain spirit and will not provide the accurate flavor.

PEACH BRANDY: Though once plentiful and popular in the region, true brandy distilled from peaches can be hard to come by these days and, if found, prohibitively expensive for batching drinks large scale. Drinks writer David Wondrich suggests this work around or "kludge": simply use two parts apple brandy and one part good-quality peach liqueur. Steer clear of all peachtree schnapps and peach-flavored brandy products, as they will ruin the authenticity of the cocktail. For those of you who want to go for the real deal, Virginia's Catoctin Creek Distillery produces a very nice peach brandy for around forty dollars for a 375-milliliter bottle.

## LIQUEURS

BENEDICTINE: A complex honey, herb and spice liqueur essential that adds the spark to the Preakness cocktail. Legend has it that the formula was developed in the early sixteenth century by Benedictine monks in France, but the modern incarnation came onto the market in the mid-nineteenth century.

CURACAO: Orange has traditionally been the most popular flavor on the sweet side of mixology. Curacao is the earliest of these cordials and originally used brandy as a base spirit. An easy substitution for original Curacao is Grand Marnier.

CHARTREUSE: Another monastery-based digestive bitter, this one still has ties to the Charthusian order that developed it as an "elixir of life" in the early seventeenth century. Two varieties exist today: green and the slightly less herbaceous, sweeter, but harder to find yellow. Both have been used somewhat interchangeably in the iconic Diamondback cocktail.

## BITTERS

An essential ingredient of most well-made cocktails today, bitters often form the subtle backnotes of the drink. Originally developed as a digestive aid, bitters fell out of favor during the "dark age" of the cocktail in the 1960s and '70s but have exploded back onto the market at the turn of the twenty-first century. There are more brands and variations out there than we have time to name, but here are some starting points for your Maryland-centric bar stash:

ABBOT'S BITTERS: Produced in Baltimore until around the 1950s, Abbott's Bitters was once as widely used as Angostura bitters are today. Legend states that it was the original bitters used in the Manhattan cocktail. Brad Parson, author of *Bitters: A Spirited History of a Classic Cure-All,* had a chance to taste a vintage bottle from the collection of Jim Meehan and described it as being "intense and spicy, with clove, cinnamon, and anise popping through on the tongue." Luckily for all of us, several reproductions have entered the market in recent years, most notably from Darcy O'Neil and Tempus Fugit Spirits.

BITTER END CHESAPEAKE BAY BITTERS: For something completely different, get your hands on Bill York's Chesapeake Bay Bitters. With notes of bay leaf, black pepper, cayenne pepper, mustard seed, celery seed, allspice, ginger, nutmeg and cardamom, it pays homage to our state obsession to all things Old Bay.

———⌘———

## A RECIPE FOR "MARYLAND BITTERS"

*If you want to get into the homemade bitters craze, try out the historically accurate recipe below from Mrs. Charles H. Gibson. With a little expense and minimal effort, you can "mass-produce" your very own authentic nineteenth-century Maryland cocktail bitters.*

One ounce gentian, one ounce cardamom seed, one ounce chamomile flowers, some dried orange peel. Bruise all together, and pour on the quantity three pints good whiskey or brandy. If preferred strain it off after it has stood some time. This is an excellent recipe and a tablespoon full in a little sugar and water is beneficial occasionally.

## SYRUPS

PINEAPPLE SYRUP: You will see this ingredient asked for quite often throughout the recipes in this book. From the punch era through the more complex apple toddies to the frozen rye, a good recipe for a pineapple-infused simple syrup will be indispensable. Please don't be tempted to use the viscous nonsense from the inside of store-bought canned pineapple—society will shun you.

———•◦◦◦•———

## PINEAPPLE-INFUSED RICH SYRUP

*Recipe adapted from Marcia Simmons and Jonas Halpern*

I cup water
½ fresh pineapple, cored and sliced into chunks
2 cups sugar

Bring the water to a boil. Let simmer for three minutes. Remove from heat and set aside to cool. Place the pineapple chunks in a large bowl and pour the cooled syrup over them. Cover and let it steep and chill overnight. Remove the pineapple chunks and reserve if desired. Yield: 2 cups.

# MARYLAND CIDER AND SPIRITS

## BLACKWATER DISTILLING

*184 Log Canoe Circle*
*Stevensville, MD 21666*
*(443) 249-3123*

Located in Stevensville, Maryland, Blackwater is the first fully licensed distillery doing business in the state since Pikesville Rye moved to Kentucky forty years ago. Also the maker of Sloop Betty Vodka, Blackwater is ramping up its rye production and should have product available soon.

## DISTILLERY LANE CIDERWORKS

*5533 Gapland Road*
*Jefferson, MD 21755*
*(301) 838-8920*
*www.distillerylaneciderworks.com*
*ciderguys@distillerylaneciderworks.com*

Situated near Burkittsville, Maryland (of *The Blair Witch Project* fame), Distillery Lane Ciderworks produces several varieties of sweet and naturally fermented hard cider from the apples grown on their family-owned farm. It was the first licensed cidery in the state of Maryland.

## FIORE WINERY AND DISTILLERY

*3026 Whiteford Road*
*Pylesville, MD 21132*
*(410) 879-4007*
*fiorewinery.com/distillery.asp*

Back in 2005, founder Mike Fiore led the lobby effort in the Maryland General Assembly to legalize distillery operations for Maryland winemakers. Though production was initially limited to 200 gallons versus the 4,000 allowed to other craft distilleries, SB858–The Maryland Winery Modernization Act increased the amount to 1,900 gallons. Today, Fiore uses the skins and seeds left over from the winemaking process— known as pomace—to produce an Italian-style digestive called grappa. It also makes several varieties of moonshine, a vodka and Limoncello.

## LINDSAY'S SOUTHSIDE MIX

*(410) 252-7747*
*www.southsides.com*

The result of Ruxton native Lindsay Hargrave's fifteen-year quest to create the "Ultimate Southside," Lindsay's Southside Mix is available in many local grocery and liquor stores. It can also be ordered online through the company website.

## LEOPOLD BROTHERS

*5285 Joliet Street*
*Denver, CO 80239*
*www.leopoldbros.com*

Scott and Todd Leopold, out of Colorado, produce a very nice Maryland-style rye that we just recently had the pleasure of sampling. Around 60 percent rye, this is certainly a less aggressive spirit in keeping with Maryland ryes of old. First released in 2011, it is 43 percent ABV or 86 proof.

## LYON DISTILLING COMPANY

*605 South Talbot Street #6*
*St Michaels, MD 21663*
*(443) 333-9181*
*lyondistilling.com*

Run by Ben Lyon and Jaime Windon, Lyon Distilling out of St. Michaels just debuted its new aged Maryland rye whiskey in February 2015, the first produced in this state since the Pikesville exodus in the 1970s. The company also produces an un-aged variety as well as several rums.

## MILLSTONE CELLARS

*2029 Monkton Road*
*Monkton, MD 21111*
*(410) 470-9818*
*www.millstonecellars.com*

Founded by the father-and-son team of Curt and Kyle Sherrer, Millstone produces a constantly changing variety of Old World–style small-batch ciders and meads, all from heirloom ingredients sourced within a one-hundred-mile radius of their nineteenth-century gristmill HQ. Be aware, the products bear the hallmarks of colonial cider making and are not for the casual Woodchuck fan.

## NEW ENGLAND DISTILLING

*26 Evergreen Drive Unit B*
*Portland, ME 04103*
*(207) 878-WSKY / (207) 878-9759*
*www.newenglanddistilling.com*

This Portland, Maine distillery was founded by Ned Wight, a descendant of Maryland Whiskey maker John Jacob Wight of Sherwood Distillery. Its Gunpowder Rye is a small-batch product, brewed from local grain and distilled in a copper-pot still. Tasting notes mention the characteristic spiciness of the Maryland style along with a "toasted malt flavor" and "big barrel character."

# PIKESVILLE RYE
# HEAVEN HILL DISTILLERY

*P.O. Box 729*
*Bardstown, KY 40004*
*(502) 348-3921*
*heavenhill.com/brand/51*

A post-Prohibition legacy brand allegedly made from an old recipe in the Maryland/Potomac style of rye whiskey, Pikesville is the "last man standing" in the rye whiskey exodus and is now made by Heaven Hill in Kentucky. Most people old enough to remember the original taste of Pikesville when it was made at Majestic Distillers, in Landsowne, state that it is definitely not the same.

Regardless of the truth, the brand, in the words of Ben Lyon of Lyon Distilling, is a "great value for the money." It offers a spicy, rich character for less than fifteen dollars in most venues. This will probably be your go-to rye whiskey for most of the recipes and should give you the best approximation of the original tastes of the drinks until Lyon and Blackwater increase production.

# PART I

### THE COLONIAL ERA

## 1631–1774

During this period, we witness the founding of the Maryland colony, the rise of the tobacco "mono-economic" and, as a result, the slower formation of towns and urban centers. Due to the dispersed population patterns brought on by the essentialness of access to water transportation, Maryland's early settlements were a patchwork series of large manors and plantations. The rich, Catholic (especially in the early years) large landowners spread out along the primary waterways, forcing those of lesser means to build slightly more inland.

While Western Europe—and, to a slightly lesser extent, New England—was enjoying beers, ales and distilled spirits, including rum and gin, cider, fruit-wines and fruit-based spirits were the common drink for Maryland colonists of all social standings. Beginning in the eighteenth century, the punch craze took hold in the Maryland colony.

## COCKTAIL TIMELINE

1600s: Native North Americans are introduced to hard spirits by European explorers and settlers. They had no prior experience with distilled beverages.

1600s: Franciscus Sylvius (or Franz de la Boe), a professor of medicine at the University of Leyden, distills spirits from grain.

1606: English Parliament passes "The Act to Repress the Odious and Loathsome Sin of Drunkenness."

1614: England imposes a levy on malt.

1630: The first attempt to impose prohibition in the New World occurs when Governor John Winthrop of Massachusetts attempted to outlaw all alcoholic beverages in Boston.

1633: Sir Kenelm Digby invents the modern hand-blown wine bottle, a much-needed replacement for the ceramic vessels used previously.

1634: Ireland begins granting licenses to the sellers of alcoholic beverages.

1651: The first mention of rum in Barbados occurs.

1652: The first distillery in the American colonies is established on Staten Island.

1657: Boston opens its first rum distillery. Within a generation, rum production will become New England's largest and most prosperous industry.

1678: Port is discovered in Portugal. Adding brandy to wine before the end of its fermentation allows it to retain some of the natural residual sugar.

1714: Gin production in England reaches two million gallons per year.

1729: English Parliament passes the Gin Control Act of 1729 to control widespread drunkenness. The law also raised taxes on the sales of alcoholic beverages.

1730: John Clarke invents the hydrometer, a device that measures the alcoholic content of beer, wine or spirits.

1731: English sailors are given the option to take their daily ration of alcohol as a pint of wine or a half pint of rum, as opposed to the traditional gallon of beer.

1733: Gin production in Holland increases 400 percent between the years 1733 and 1792. In England, Parliament repeals the ineffectual Gin Control Act. A new act would be passed in 1736 to raise gin prices to a higher level than the poor could afford.

# MARYLAND TIMELINE

1608: John Smith explores the Chesapeake Bay.

1631: Ken Island is established as a trading post by Virginians.

1632: George Calvert, the first Baron Baltimore, dies, and his son Cecilius is granted the charter to the Maryland colony.

1634: The *Ark* and the *Dove* land at St. Clements.

1642: The English Civil War pits Royalists loyal to the king against the forces of Parliament led by Oliver Cromwell.

1649: The Act of Toleration is passed in Maryland, guaranteeing religious freedom.

1662: Maryland enacts a law to promote the establishment of inns with a monopoly on alcohol sales within a specific geographic area. It was intended to promote inn keeping, brewing, distilling, travel and commerce.

1689: Lord Baltimore's proprietorship is overthrown, and Maryland becomes a Royal colony in 1691.

1715: The Proprietorship is restored.

1729: Baltimore Town is founded.

1756–63: Britain battles France as the Seven Years' War rages worldwide. The conflict on the North American continent is known as the French and Indian War.

# CHAPTER 1

# ALCOHOL IN COLONIAL MARYLAND

## THE FOUNDING OF MARYLAND

In 1634, English settlers—mostly male indentured servants—landed in what is now St. Mary's City after a three-month journey across the Atlantic. Many of them perished a short while after their arrival. Even though they had found safe harbor, the settlers were confronted by a vast, virgin forest and struggled to bend this new environment to their English way of life in order to bring some framework of stability to their new lives.

In the years prior to the founding, George Calvert, former secretary of state to King James I, had been involved in the English colonization efforts in Ireland, North Carolina and Newfoundland, but upon his conversion to Catholicism, he was forced to resign his official offices. As a reward for his years of service, the king elevated Calvert to the title of Baron Baltimore. Since he now required a new stream of revenue, Calvert was granted proprietorship of the territory to the north of the existing Virginia colony. In 1632, George Calvert died, and the right to found the Maryland colony passed to his eldest son, Cecilius.

Under the proprietorship, the Calverts held near kingly power over the colony. They could raise a personal army for defense of the land, as well as build fortifications. They held sway over all trade matters and could both impose and collect all tariffs and duties. In legal matters, they could establish courts, grant lands and titles and found townships. For all of these powers,

Cecil Calvert. From Leonard Magruder's *Maryland; Stories of Her People and of Her History* (1905). *Archive.org*

the Calverts annually owed the Crown two Indian arrows and one-fifth of any precious metals found within the colony.

On November 22, 1633, around 130 colonists set sail from the Isle of Wight aboard the four-hundred-ton English merchant vessel *Ark* and the forty-ton pinnace *Dove*. Hired by Cecil Calvert, Second Lord Baltimore,

The *Ark* and the *Dove* leaving from the Isle of Wight. *Archive.org.*

the vessels, their passengers and supplies set forth to found the new colony of Maryland, the charter for which Cecil had acquired upon the death of his father, George, in April of the previous year. Three days after departure, the two ships became separated, and the *Dove*, last seen flying signs of distress, disappeared into a storm. The two vessels wouldn't be reunited until rendezvousing in Barbados late in January. The *Ark* would be assailed by a second, more violent three-day storm on November 29, and its mainsail would be split. The crew members were forced to make hasty repairs, but fortunately, it would be the last of the foul weather encountered during the voyage.

Colonists to the new land north of the Potomac River and on either side of the Chesapeake Bay were brought over by the *Ark* and the *Dove*. The *Ark*, the main vessel of the voyage, was, by most accounts, large for the time, but at a maximum, its dimensions were a mere 110 feet in length and 40 feet at its widest point. Although scant few of the Catholic gentlemen aboard may have had modest cabins, the vast majority of colonists—mainly Protestant indentured servants and a mere handful of women—were confined below deck in the claustrophobic belly of the *Ark*, where they endured "water-soaked bedding" and nothing even resembling privacy for the duration of

*The Founding of Maryland. Library of Congress.*

the four-month journey. On top of this, the average passenger was subjected to a monotonous diet of ship's biscuits and beer, supplemented on occasion by a bit of dried meet and cheese. Despite the harsh conditions, only twelve fatalities accrued during the trip, and these, oddly enough, were due to overconsumption of Christmas wine.

Sailing up the Potomac, the *Ark* landed on St. Clement Island on March 5, 1634, where Leonard Calvert, leading the expedition for his older brother, entreated for the right to settle with the local Native American tribes. The colonists chose the site of what would become St. Mary's City for the first settlement, and on March 25, the Jesuit priest accompanying the voyage offered a mass of Thanksgiving. This date is celebrated to this day as Maryland Day.

## MARYLAND ALCOHOL CULTURE

For the average Maryland colonist, habits and views on the consumption of alcohol were rooted in the drinking conditions of the mother country. Though their goal was to reproduce the societal model they were familiar

Old St. Mary's. *Archive.org*

with back in England, the new Marylanders had to adapt to their new local environment. With a mixture of English tradition and colonial innovation, they would forge an entirely new drinking culture for a new land.

During the colonial era, alcohol was an unavoidable necessity of life, and the first Marylanders came out of England with a pattern of heavy consumption. Back in England, due largely to low-quality water supplies, drinking was the norm, and soon low-alcohol beers and ales all but replaced water as the daily beverage for the ordinary citizen. Most English adults of the time drank a minimum of one gallon of ale or cider a day. Even children under the age of ten commonly consumed nearly half a quart of the same beverages during mealtime.

The colonial Marylanders' dependence on alcohol was far greater even than that of their English relations, as it brought much-needed calories to their often meager diets. Even in the New World, clean drinkable water was hard to come by. The warm climate of the Chesapeake region fostered the growth of deadly bacteria, and many waterways were already infested with mosquito larvae. Wells dug by the colonists were often too shallow, and many inhabitants fell victim to diseases like typhoid fever and malaria.

In the early days of Maryland settlement, transatlantic trade with England—and, to a smaller extent, the rest of the European powers—flowed freely, and the well-off gladly paid out to import both beers and spirits from back home. For the majority of inhabitants, drink was "one of the few pleasures in their lives," and the average adult male drank constantly throughout the day. A pick-me-up upon waking would be followed by another drink at midmorning, and some form of alcohol would be consumed with lunch and then again late in the afternoon. Finally, the day would be capped off with a final drink at suppertime.

By itself, trade with England proved insufficient to meet the sheer demand, and if available, alcohol was at such a high price that the average Marylander could scarcely afford to pay for his daily drink. This fact illuminated the dire need for the domestic production of alcohol. Unfortunately for Marylanders, the beer and ales they had grown so accustomed to back home required a large surplus of grain that they would never be able to produce—let alone part with—for some time. Upon landfall the colonists were faced with heavy forestation, and the efforts required to clear enough land to grow grain proved a difficult and costly undertaking. Add to this the need to construct malt houses, and the entire process of brewing beer would prove to be an overly extravagant undertaking. There was some trade with the local Native American tribes for hominy and other fermentable grains but not on any scale to facilitate sufficient beer production. Maryland would lag behind in grain production until increased slave trade in the eighteenth century.

Due to irregular immigration and the scattered pattern of settlement created by the dependence on the tobacco economy, the alcohol production of eighteenth-century Maryland was closer to that of sixteenth-century England than to New England or the Middle Colonies of the same era. Colonial Maryland was rather late in the development of towns (most early settlements were large manors or plantations), and as a result, there were usually no stores or taverns from which to buy drink, so if you wanted alcohol, you were forced to make your own. While some of their more advanced neighbors were enjoying a heyday of distilled spirits and hopped beers, the settlers of the early Chesapeake were limited to beverages fermented from apples, pears, peaches and persimmons. What little ale was produced was brewed from corn and molasses rather than the traditional oats and barley that were especially in short supply. In especially desperate times, the colonists even consumed a concoction made up of molasses and water.

# CIDER

From the seventeenth century onward, nearly half of the Maryland population could be lumped into the category of "small planter"—that is, owning a mere one hundred or two hundred acres and growing crops for a living. Most of these households worked the land themselves assisted only by two to three indentured servants or, later, slaves.

Easily produced from apples, cider (the nonalcoholic version being referred to as "sweet cider) was by far the most prevalent beverage in the dawn of English society on the Chesapeake. Once the fruit was harvested, it was pounded in a trough and the pomace drained off (the first hand-cranked cider mills wouldn't appear until the 1740s), fermented—sweet cider would do so on its own rather easily—in some vessel or another and served once the alcohol had reached a level to kill off all of the yeast. In addition to its mildly alcoholic effects, cider also provided a source of certain nutritional elements otherwise sadly missing from the early colonial diet.

The cider season commonly began with the August apple harvest, with the racking of the final barrels usually occurring in March. Again, due to cider's lack of long-term shelf life, supplies would quickly dwindle in the spring and summer months.

In England, from the third century forward, the task of producing the family's alcohol supply fell to the "fairer sex," lumped into the duties of running the household. Aristocratic ladies would provide instructions to their servants, but those of lesser means had to perform the task personally. Generally, the efforts of the lady of the house were able to fulfill their family's alcohol needs from late July through December, dependent on the harvest season for the fruit to be fermented.

Of all of the fruit available to the colonists, the apple proved the most important to the settlers of the early Chesapeake. Though initially hampered by such factors as lack of bees for pollination and the short lives of the trees, determined planting caused the sheer number of varieties to grow at an astounding rate. By the dawn of the eighteenth century, the initial hurdles were overcome and the apple became an essential part of the colonial diet. Of the types of apples, there were sixteen separate varieties for cooking or just eating as is, nineteen suited for desserts—mostly pies—and six specifically suited for the production of what we would refer to today as "hard cider." One of these cider-specific types was shipped over to Jamestown almost immediately after settlement to spur production.

Soon, farmers and tavern owners were producing at such a volume that they were able to sell off their surplus alcohol to their neighbors and gain cash to spend on hard spirits and other European trade goods. Eventually, demand would grow so great that some were even able to support their families solely off this additional income. The short shelf life of cider cut out any possibilities of exportation, however, and production was kept small at the hyper-local level.

In 1756, Elizabeth Brook, writing from Annapolis to her son Charles Carroll, away at school in Europe, had this to say about fruit production in Maryland: "This place…is greatly improved, a fine, flourishing orchard with a variety of choice fruit." Charles Carroll of Annapolis and his son annually put away vast quantities of cider for their family and servants.

By 1775, the Carrolls were storing away over twenty-two thousand gallons of "cyder" for the year to come. In the 1790s, Captain John O'Donnell, the founder of Canton—named after his favorite port of call—settled in Baltimore and planted orchards of red peaches on his 2,500-acre estate. He hoped the venture would allow him to produce brandy for trade, but unfortunately, he ultimately met with little success.

# WINE

From the seventeenth to eighteenth century, Madeira, a Portuguese fortified wine known for its ability to survive and even improve in a ship's hold over the long transatlantic voyages, was the most popular and important wine in British North America. The secret to Madeira's resiliency—much like that of its cousin, port—was a small addition of cane sugar distillate, which stabilized the wine and prevented spoilage at sea. The time spent in the heat and choppy seas during a voyage was actually shown to artificially age the wine, transforming the taste completely into one that was highly sought after by American colonists. By 1750, the sugar-based spirit was swapped out, and the new taste of brandy-fortified Madeira just made it all the more desirable. Everyone from Washington to Jefferson to Franklin and Adams were huge Madeira fans. It was even used to toast the signing of the Declaration of Independence.

In order to further encourage colonial alcohol production, Lord Baltimore established over three hundred acres of vineyards in 1662, but nearly all of American grape planting attempts met with failure, as the imported European varietals were no match for the diseases and pests of the New World. At the household level, however, colonists were busy at work creating fruit-based wines out of whatever they could lay their hands on, and recipes for cherry, lemon, gooseberry, blackberry and elderberry wine soon appeared. By 1705, a traveler to the Maryland colony remarked on the "abundance of fruits of all sorts as aple Peare Cherry quinces in great quantities and innumerable Quantities Peaches to that degree that they knock downe Bushells att a time for their hogs besides what vast quantities they stil and make very good spirit off nott much inferior to Brandy."

## DISTILLED SPIRITS

Because of the popularity of cider and other fruit fermentations, small-scale distillation of apple and peach brandies soon followed in the houses of wealthier planters. Lacking the means to purchase the often expensive equipment, small planters often had to purchase surplus spirits from their richer neighbors to make it through to the next cidering season. Cider would

Pot still. *Library of Congress.*

easily undergo freeze-distillation if left outside during the winter months, as the unfrozen alcohol was skimmed away off the ice, but proper apple brandy and peach brandy also began to appear in small quantities, especially in the southern colonies like Maryland. Though they required a greater degree of equipment and knowledge, distillation ultimately made good economic sense since the spirits kept longer, were more potent—thereby taking up less space per serving—and, as a result, were more easily transported. No single spirit capitalized on these factors more than rum, allowing it to become the dominant distilled spirit of the age.

In the English-controlled Caribbean islands, rum, a byproduct of the sugar refinement process, was created from molasses—essentially industrial waste—and North American colonists either imported it legally through British channels or smuggled cheaper sources out of French and Spanish possessions. Rum was itself a powerful economic force, and the demand for molasses as a raw material drove trade. It is thought that the colonial American adult male consumed, on average, three pints of rum a week.

Though generally inferior in quality to its Caribbean counterpart, American rum—often referred to as Medford rum in New England—could be produced domestically for almost half the cost. By the 1770s, there were approximately 140 distilleries dotting the eastern seaboard and producing almost five million gallons of rum a year, compared to the less than 4 million gallons of ready-made Caribbean rum imported into the thirteen colonies in the same time span.

## MEDICINAL PURPOSES

Since its introduction, alcohol was believed to possess medicinal properties, and colonial Maryland held to these ideas that drink was good for your health. After all, alcohol kept the body warm (keeping work crews going during the harvest), eased digestion after a heavy meal and cured or lessened the perceived severity of a number of other ailments. Rye whiskey was thought to ease a sore throat, hot brandy eased the suffering of cholera patients and rum-soaked cherries were commonly prescribed for the common cold. For more serious matters, rum could serve as anesthesia during dental work and surgical procedures. Even the pains of a woman in labor could be alleviated by the administering of a shot of whatever spirits one had at hand.

# LAWS

*Not drunk is he who from the floor, can rise again and still drink more,*
*But drunk is he who prostrate lies without the power to drink or rise.*
—*Justice Askham, in defense of his own charges of public drunkenness*

The colony of Maryland was at the forefront of issuing laws governing liquor in the English New World. While most of them reflected previous English laws, at least in spirit, there were also measures enacted that showed a higher degree of concern for the health of the individual as far as the consumption of alcohol was concerned. Early legislation was primarily aimed at limiting disorderly conduct and promoting peaceful social environments. Though sales of alcohol on Sunday were banned—as they continue to be in some counties of the state—there were no limits on the actual amount of alcohol that could be consumed by the individual on any other day of the week.

By 1638, the penalty for public drunkenness was a fine of 30 pounds of tobacco—the common currency of the day—but by 1643, the fine skyrocketed to 120 pounds and, after three infractions, the loss of voting rights for one year. In reality, there were very few actual cases brought to trial, and most of them involved either violence or the destruction of physical property as well. All in all, colonial Maryland was a society that encouraged drinking and, in most cases, forgave or turned a blind eye to frequent drunken behavior, provided no one was hurt by it or no one's property was damaged severely.

So what constituted drunkenness? This was largely determined on an individual basis and usually depended on the person's ability to function normally and whether or not it hurt his job performance or caused a public safety issue. Once again, Justice Askham has a ruling on this, stating, "A man is never drunk if he can got out of the carts way when it is coming towards him." In addition, there was a commonly held belief in the rest of colonial America that excessive drinking and outright drunkenness were caused by a person's insufficient willpower and that sobriety was a simple matter of mental fortitude as you had to "want" to remain sober. The concept of addiction was a ways off.

## LIFE, DEATH AND ALCOHOL

Unlike many of the other English colonies, Maryland, known for its religious freedoms, was also decidedly egalitarian in the distribution of alcohol. From the Catholic, cavalier elite to the Protestant indentured servants, all societal classes had access to alcoholic drink of some form, and there are few, if any, accounts stating that even the humblest of citizens were forced to that poor man's drink of last resort: water. In fact, the contracts governing indentured servitude usually mandated that employers provide adequate drink along with sufficient food, apparel and lodging for their charges.

Maryland colonists were never at a loss for a reason to drink, and the alcohol flowed freely during holidays, weddings, births and even funerals. While men and women frequently drank together within the home, away from it, social drinking was divided along gender lines. Female drinking was usually confined to the indoor sphere, centered around sewing circles or births, where the mother-to-be was expected to have cakes and alcohol available for the visiting neighbor women. The men drank everywhere else, even at church services, during court proceedings and while voting.

Rum was often the drink of choice for funerals, and tales of mass consumption were regularly reported, as wealthy planters were keen to drink to the memory of even the poorest of their neighbors, provided the estate could support the alcohol tab. Like cider, rum was on occasion "mulled" with spices. Take, for instance, the account for the funeral of one William Drewry, a rich man from Anne Arundel County. When Drewry was laid to rest in the latter part of the seventeenth century, the damage toll was fifty-five gallons of cider mulled with brandy, sugar and spices consumed. We won't even mention the colossal dinner served that required the active service of two maids. On the opposite end of the scale was Loling Moloney, a poor man who in death possessed nothing but "the clothes on his back" and one "sorry horse." Though he had neither creditors nor kin left to mourn him, Moloney's "estate," after the funeral fees, still had enough to buy—presumably for the undertakers and gravediggers—a gallon of rum "to mark his passing."

# CHAPTER 2

# THE FLOWING BOWL

*One of sour, two of sweet, three of strong, four of weak.*
—*Barbadian rhyme*

## PUNCH

In the early days of colonization, rum was usually enjoyed neat, straight out of the bottle or in a dram cup. But even with the considerable uptick in domestic alcohol production, the colony was still relatively dependent on Europe for hard liquor up into the eighteenth century. Costs were still high, so anyone who was able to obtain hard spirits such as rum or grape brandy usually cut or "lengthened" them with the addition of fruit juices and spices. Not only did it improve flavor, it also increased the number of guests you were able to serve with a given amount of liquor. From the middle of the seventeenth century to the dawn of the cocktail era in the 1850s, punch was the undisputed king of drinks in the English-speaking world. At the time, the term "punch"—derived from either the Hindustani word for "five" or the English word "puncheon" (a large cask used for wine storage)—was used to describe one specific drink and was not the wide classification we have today stretching all the way from Planter's Punch to the sherbet and ginger ale abomination your grandparents tried to pass off as a party drink. Punch originated sometime around the early to mid-seventeenth century and was first common among the sailors and traders of the British East India Company. The first printed mention comes from a 1632 letter from R. Addams to T. Colley warning of the dangers of over consumption: "I hop you will keep a good house together and drinke punch by no allowanc."

In contrast to Addams's ominous warning, punch is described as a "subtle and delightful blend of fine and often exotic liquors, softened with water, brightened with freshly squeezed juices of citrus fruit, sweetened with pure cane sugar and touched with rare spices," and it was the first drink utilizing hard spirits as a base that grabbed public attention in such a grand manner.

Early recipes for punch usually adhered to the five-ingredient rule: lemon or lime, sugar, spice—usually nutmeg or tea, but occasionally as exotic as ambergris—liquor of some kind and water. Of the liquors originally used in punch, Batavia Arrak—a hot, aromatic, rice-and-molasses distillate imported from the Dutch East Indies—was the most popular, but as punch moved from its scruffy sailor origins and into polite society, rum and French brandy soon found their way into the bowl as well. By the 1690s, punch was fully respectable, and the wealthy of both genders now gathered around the punch bowl for entertainment as the local punch master showed off his array of specialized tools.

By the mid-seventeenth century, dinners and society functions made a "showy fashion" of their alcoholic drinks and punches, and their often hard-to-obtain fruit juices and spices conjured up images of exotic lands to the east. As English convention mixed with the colonial innovative streak, a veritable punch mania set in. This obsession was hardly confined to the upper classes: households across the economic spectrum suddenly saw an increase in the assortment of serving wares and often bizarre paraphernalia required to keep up with the craze. Attention to every last detail in proper punch preparation proved to be a measure of your hospitality.

Here is a very basic punch recipe from Marietta Gibson's *Maryland and Virginia Cookbook*. Though published in 1894, the recipe is in keeping with a relatively modest eighteenth-century rum punch:

> *One gallon New England rum, one pint lemon juice, juice and peel of two oranges, let stand twenty-four hours, then add four pounds sugar, one pint strong tea, four pints water. It can be bottled in a few days.*

The eighteenth century was a hard-drinking but innovative time, and punch was the drink of choice for the Enlightenment Era. In 1708, English poet Ebenezer Cook records our first local reference to the excesses of punch consumption. While traveling in Maryland, he noticed "a herd of Planters on the ground, O'er-whelmed with Punch." As punch makers got more adept in their craft, the five-ingredient rule was broken, and recipes became ever more elaborate with the addition of fruit syrups (pineapple seemed especially popular), fancy liqueurs and even champagne. Spirits writer David Wondrich asserts that this later development in the era of punch making provided the original proving ground for mixology. The recipe below illustrates one of these more elaborate creations. The "bishop"—a traditional eighteenth-century holiday libation—belongs to a punch-like classification of drinks, English in origin, named after the church hierarchy. For example, a bishop was made with port and an archbishop with claret, while a cardinal would be topped with champagne and the pope used burgundy as a base. This Harford County version is a bit more rustic, playing hard and fast with the rules and omitting even the port itself:

―⧙⧙⧙―

## FARMER'S BISHOP, A CHRISTMAS PUNCH

*Recipe by Amelia Pinkeney D. Lurman, Harford County. Adapted from*
Maryland's Way: The Hammond-Harwood House Cook Book.

6 oranges
whole cloves [exact number not mentioned, but a little goes a long way]
sugar to taste
1 quart apple brandy
½ gallon sweet cider
cinnamon, whole allspice and nutmeg to taste

Cut oranges in half and stick skins full of whole cloves. Bake in oven until juice begins to run. Remove to bowl that can be kept hot. Add sugar to taste and pour over them 1 quart apple brandy. Light brandy and after it has burned a few seconds, extinguish by pouring over the cider. Place bowl over a low flame or at back of stove. Add pinch of cinnamon, whole allspice and nutmeg (go easy on spices). Stir mixture until hot. It should be kept hot while being served but must never reach boiling. Serves about 24. This punch was served in the countryside when the Bishop was expected. The receipt said, "Add brandy to the amount of the capacity of the Bishop."

# THE PEGGY STEWART TEA PARTY

On October 19, 1774, ten months after the Sons of Liberty threw 342 chests of tea into the waters of Boston Harbor, Annapolis held its own fiery tea party. Four days prior, the brig *Peggy Stewart*—named for the daughter of the owner, Alexander Stewart—arrived in Annapolis harbor with fifty-three indentured servants. Among its cargo was seventeen chests, nearly a ton in all, of untaxed tea belonging to Thomas Charles Williams & Co. When the brig had set out from England in the summer of 1774, the tea had been disguised as chests of cloth in an effort to avoid the tax. The plan promptly failed when the ship's captain, Richard Jackson, who had not been told about the cargo and was rightfully wary of a smuggling charge, panicked and identified the tea on his customs declaration before leaving England.

When the ship finally arrived, the citizens of Annapolis saw the act as an affront to the resolution passed on July 22 calling for a boycott of trade with England and the colonies of the West Indies and demanded action. In an effort to placate the crowd, Alexander Stewart and the Williams brothers

The Peggy Stewart House. *Library of Congress.*

offered to remove the chests of the hated tea from the vessel, burn them and put out a public apology, but the enraged citizenry would not be appeased. It was at this point that Stewart ordered the ship run aground, where he would personally set it to the torch.

In the years following the Peggy Stewart Affair, the incident, often referred to as the "Annapolis Tea Party," is now remembered as an act of patriotism and resistance on the part of the citizens of Annapolis.

—⁓—

## PEGGY STEWART TEA PUNCH

*Recipe by Mrs. J. Pierre Bernard, Peggy Stewart House, Annapolis. Adapted from* Maryland's Way: The Hammond-Harwood House Cook Book.

3 pints cold water
8 teaspoonful best tea
thin rind and juice of 8 lemons
1½ pounds cut sugar
1 quart rum
½ pint whiskey

Let tea boil, leaving lemon and rind in. While on the fire throw in pulp of lemons (having squeezed out juice). When boiled sufficiently, pour off into a bowl. Put in sugar, juice of the lemons and add rum and whiskey if you like. Pour over ice to serve.

# PART II

# THE GOTHIC AGE

## 1775–1859

The "Gothic Age of American drinking," a phrase coined by Baltimore's own H.L. Mencken, refers to the years between the Revolutionary War and the Civil War. At the start, punch was still at the height of its appeal in the new Republic, and by the end, the United States was on the cusp of the golden age of the American cocktail. The outbreak of hostilities between Britain and its thirteen former colonies resulted in the disruption of rum and molasses trade, and the resultant rise of rye whiskey changed the American palate forever. Soon, rye became a matter of national pride.

In the 1770s, the Wilderness Road stretched from Virginia north over the Allegheny Mountains and opened up a vital trade route. In 1791, in response to the Distilled Spirits Tax, the Whiskey Rebellion broke out in the western rye-producing areas of Maryland and, to a more violent degree, in Pennsylvania. It was put down personally by President Washington, leading an army larger than that of the Revolution.

The year 1806 saw the first printed mention of the cocktail in the *Balance and Columbian Repository* out of Hudson, New York: "Cocktail is a stimulating liquor, composed of spirits of any kind, sugar, water and bitters—and is vulgarly called a bittered sling." Who created the cocktail? What was the origin of the name? No one knows for certain, and various tales are as farfetched as a fictional barmaid poaching feathers from her Tory neighbor to place in the drinks of Continental soldiers. H.L. Mencken, who admitted that the origin of the word was most likely lost to history, surmised that it could be the combinations of the words for tap for a keg and the dregs at the bottom of the barrel, which were commonly mixed together with other barrels and sold at discount.

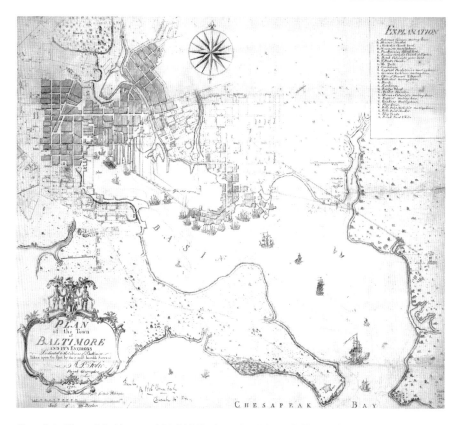

*Plan of the Town of Baltimore and It's* [sic] *Environs* (1792) by A.P. Folie. *Library of Congress.*

In the 1830s, ice harvesting operations began, and the price of ice began to fall to affordable levels, allowing it to be enjoyed year round.

In the larger world, innovations and inventions provided the essential building blocks to herald the oncoming age of the cocktail. In 1786, Antonio Camparo created the first commercially produced Italian-style (aka sweet) vermouth. Joseph Noilly's French Vermouth (aka dry) emerged in Marseille, France, at the beginning of the nineteenth century. Drinks more resembling what we would generically term cocktails begin to emerge, like the Tom Collins at Limmer's hotel in London and the Tom and Jerry, popularized by Pierce Egan—supposedly as a publicity stunt to promote his book featuring characters of the same name—in the 1820s. Soon after, Robert Stein invented the continuous still, adding much greater efficiency to the distillation process. It was improved upon four years later by Aeneas Coffey's patent still. These innovations brought on the age of blended Scotch whisky.

## COCKTAIL TIMELINE

1774–83: The American Revolutionary War takes place.

1777: George Washington writes to John Hancock speaking of "benefits arising from the moderate use of strong Liquor" for army morale.

1781: Corks become the common bottle stopper, enabling bottle aging and cellaring of wine.

1789: The first Kentucky whiskey is distilled by the Baptist minister Reverend Elijah Craig.

1791: The Distilled Spirits Tax of 1791 imposes a tax on all distilled spirits produced in the United States.

1792: Absinthe is invented in Switzerland by Dr. Pierre Ordinaire.

1803: This year brings the first recorded instance of the mint julep.

1804: British physician Thomas Trotter suggests for the first time that chronic drunkenness is actually a disease.

1805: Absinthe appears in France, creating a popularity that will last for decades. Soon after, the spirit arrives in New Orleans and other French colonies.

1810: Oktoberfest becomes an annual event in Munich, Germany.

1826: The first temperance society is formed in the United States.

1830: Aeneas Coffey invents the patent still, improving the 1826 continuous still design by Robert Stein.

1830: Ice harvesting begins.

1859: The Sazerac, allegedly the first cocktail of American origin, is invented in New Orleans.

## MARYLAND TIMELINE

1778: Baltimore's first restaurant, William Stinson's, opens at Market (now Baltimore) and South Streets.

1783: Annapolis became the nation's capital from November 1783 until August.

1806: The Historic National Road, which will stretch from Maryland to the Ohio River, is commissioned as America's first federally funded highway. Construction begins in Cumberland five years later.

1813: The British raid Havre de Grace during the War of 1812.

1814: After torching the White House, British general Robert Ross leads five thousand troops north. "I'll dine tonight in Baltimore—or in hell," he is quoted as saying. Oddly enough, General Ross never actually dines in Baltimore.

1837: The *Baltimore Sun* newspaper begins publication.

1842: On his tour of the United States, Charles Dickens praises Baltimore's cuisine above all others. Reportedly, he also sips his first mint julep here.

1844: The Maryland Historical Society is incorporated as one of the first historical heritage societies in America.

1845: The school that would become the U.S. Naval Academy is established at Fort Severn, Annapolis, with seven professors and forty midshipmen. Franklin Buchanan is named the first superintendent.

1849: Edgar Allan Poe dies while traveling in Baltimore. He is laid to rest in the Westminster Burying Ground in Baltimore.

1856: The term "mixologist" appears in print for the first time.

## CHAPTER 3

# THE MARYLAND
# APPLE TODDY

## TODDIES

From the middle of the eighteenth century to the dawn of the twentieth, the toddy, a versatile and resilient precursor of the cocktail, dominated the landscape of American drinking. Requiring none of the more perishable components or overwrought recipes of its forebear, the punch, the basic recipe for the toddy consisted of a base spirit—usually rum—as well as sugar (as much as you could stand) and water. It could be served hot or cold and, with the addition or subtraction of water, could be made as strong or as weak as the consumer desired.

Just like today, the toddy was often prescribed for various eighteenth-century maladies. In 1750s, a preadolescent Charles Willson Peale asked an Annapolis doctor (of obvious Scottish descent) which drink produced the most health benefits:

> When a boy, the jeers of my companions could not force me to follow some practices, the forerunners of vice and misery: hence I conclude. I have been constitutionally obstinate, a disposition that requires perhaps more then my years of experience to direct to advantage—so that my whole life has afforded nothing but a series of experiments.—At an early period I asked Doctor Hamilton senior (an eminent Physician near Annapolis), what is the best drink for health? "Toddy mun," the

*Toddy at the Cheshire Cheese*, by William Henry Boucher. *Library of Congress.*

*old Gentleman replied in his Caledonian dialect: "the spirit must ha [sic] something to act on, and therefore acts on the sugar and does nae injury to the stomach."*

## THE APPLE TODDY

*Egg-nog [sic] and apple toddy are the standard mixed strong drinks of Christmas in Baltimore now, as they have always been. The higher-priced saloons dispense champagne punches and other gilt-edged concoctions, but it is safe to say that nearly every liquor saloon had its twin bowls of egg-nog [sic] and apple toddy on Christmas Eve. They are seductive drinks, and the fact that Baltimore today, with its great population, does not imbibe as much as did the much smaller Baltimore of 15 or 20 years ago is considered a subject for congratulation.*

—Baltimore Sun, *December 26, 1888*

Around the 1780s, a variant of the toddy appeared, even more popular in the Chesapeake region than the original: the apple toddy. Long sought after as a "solace in winter," the apple toddy for a time became a true symbol of American patriotism, and Maryland had a special fondness for the drink that stretched into the early decades of the 1900s.

Prior to Prohibition, the apple toddy was the equivalent of fireworks on the Fourth of July for the Maryland Christmas season. Some trace the origin of this combination of baked apples, spices and various brown spirits to the Calvert family, but the apple toddy was common throughout mid-Atlantic states during the mid- to late eighteenth century. Unlike the toddies commonly found today, "Gothic Age" toddies could be served either hot or cold, the Maryland apple toddy being of the latter style. As with the mint julep and the much later martini, there are many strongly held opinions regarding the creation of a proper Maryland apple toddy. Apples: boil or bake? Spirits: rum, French brandy, applejack, rye or a mix? Maud Bomberger provided her family's recipe from Weldon Manor near South Mountain in her 1907 cookbook:

> *About Thanksgiving Day take ½ dozen large, smooth, and good cooking apples, and roast them until they burst open. While hot mash them—skin, seeds, and all—and pour on them ½ gallon good apple brandy. Add sugar and seal tight in a stone jar until Christmas Day. Weaken with water to taste. If the apples have not all been reduced to pulp, serve what is left of them with the toddy. As old Malachi said, "Take a little of de apple. Dat's whar de real spression ob de toddy is."*

A letter to the editor of the *Baltimore Sun*—quoting this recipe—said it is a "nectar fit for the gods" and provides a very good starter recipe for a homemade apple toddy, devoid of the spices and flavored liqueurs called for in later recipes.

In Maryland, the apple toddy is served from the punch bowl—a convention the state held on to publicly much longer than the rest of the nation—doled out by the silver ladleful and drunk from common table glasses, each with a teaspoon so as to stir back anything that may settle to the bottom. An additional feature of the Maryland-style apple toddy is that it is normally aged to mellow out the taste. One month is the norm in printed recipes—most ladies of the house would set their toddies down around Thanksgiving—but sometimes bars and social clubs would cellar their stashes for one year or more. One holiday soiree advertised a three-year-old apple toddy as the highlight of the evening to lure in paying customers.

In antebellum Baltimore, it was common to host open houses on Christmas Day, and no respectable family was without their dual bowls of apple toddy and eggnog. Not to be confined to the Christmas season, apple toddy was even served at one of the inaugural balls for the ultimately short-lived presidency of President Zachary Taylor in March 1849.

By 1873, we get a more elaborate rendition of the apple toddy from Mrs. B.C. Howard (aka Jane Grant Howard), the daughter-in-law to Maryland Revolutionary War hero John Eager Howard, in *Fifty Years in a Maryland Kitchen*. You may notice that the drink has now taken on many of the components and characteristics of punches:

## JANE GRANT HOWARD'S APPLE TODDY

Eight well baked red-streaked apples.
One pint each:
Peach brandy.
Jamaica spirits.
Santa Crux rum.
Powdered sugar.
Four quarts of boiling water.
Ten cloves; ten allspice; six blades of mace.
Half a nutmeg, grated.
Half a tea-spoonful of ground ginger.
Two table-spoonfuls of pine-apple syrup.
Four slices of preserved pine-apple.

When cold, strain, and keep in a cold place for two or three weeks.

In addition to its presence on the home sideboard, the apple toddy was omnipresent throughout holiday celebrations at Maryland's prominent social clubs. The Baltimore Club, the Athenaeum Club, the Maryland Club and the South River club all boasted about the superiority of their apple toddies, all of which might feature wildly different recipes by this point. Apple toddy was popular with the hunt club crowd and was present at the Christmas

Athenaeum Club, Baltimore. Historic American Buildings Survey. *Library of Congress.*

The Maryland Club, Baltimore. Historic American Buildings Survey. *Library of Congress.*

Eve open houses at both the Elkridge Club and the Green Spring Valley Club. By this time, rye whiskey was largely displacing the traditional rum and brandy mixtures, but orange liqueur, Madeira and even champagne found their ways into the elegantly iced toddy bowl. The Baltimore Club's famous recipe is as follows:

> [T]*ake four dozen roasted apples and add it* [to] *three pints of apple brandy. A half pint of peach brandy is poured in and one pint of Curocoa. A quart of champagne—any good kind will do—comes next with three pounds of sugar and three lemons, sliced thin. Six pints of cognac must be available to make it perfect, together with a quart of Jamaican rum. It is kept some time before being served.*

The South River Club's recipe, recounted below by Forbes Calhoun in the 1960s and originally from *Maryland's Way: The Hammond-Harwood House Cook Book*, was the oddball in the group, one of the few establishments that served its signature toddy hot:

> *Bake 6 large apples, cored but not peeled. Place in bottom of 3 gallon stone crock on hearth before a hot fire. Add ½ gallon boiling water, ½ pound sugar and let simmer for ½ hour, turning crock occasionally. Then add 1 gallon apple juice slowly, 1 gallon Maryland Rye whiskey and 1 quart Jamaican rum. Keep turning over with ladle and turning crock so as not to heat too much on one side. When it has simmered for 1 hour add skins of 6 lemons cut in long spirals, ½ ounce whole cloves, ¼ ounce stick cinnamon, ¼ ounce ground nutmeg. Allow to simmer for a couple of hours. Serve in cups which are first dipped in hot water. This toddy was made at the South River Club for the winter breakfasts. It should serve about 25 moderate drinkers.*

For the uninitiated, the apple toddy can be quite the potent drink, especially if undiluted: "If they were from a land where apple toddy was unknown they took the poisoned glass smilingly and sipped the toddy daintily." Take for example in 1899, when the Maryland Fifth Regiment went on the road and traveled to New York for the unveiling of the Ulysses S. Grant monument. To mark the special occasion, officers of the regiment carried along with them several gallons of good old Maryland apple toddy to share with the officers of the other units. Apparently, it "did fearful execution." Some even say that an entire New York regiment was taken out of commission for a day. By the 1920s, some were so fearful of the potency of the apple toddy that many households limited each guest to one glass of toddy, even though they were usually given free rein to consume as much sherry and port as they pleased.

The apple toddy's fortunes waned once again as the temperance movement began to take hold around the turn of the century. Several articles demonized both the toddy and the classic eggnog, blaming them for the drunken binges engaged in by young men of the day, as it was traditional to go "calling" upon various houses, enjoying a drink at each before moving on to the next. The *Baltimore Sun* writers were quick to mourn, asking, "Have the festive eggnog, the seductive apple toddy and the sorrow-dispelling Tom and Jerry been relegated to the background or become the sport of Willie boys? Alas it would seem so, and another tradition of the good old days appears to be on the point of disappearing."

The article observed that sales were flagging overall with these traditional drinks and that "callow youths," flush with their Christmas money, were ordering them "as they would buy ice-cream," seeking to raise hell around town and be "real devils." Some things never do change. Other than that, only the occasional "old-timer" would stop in to have a glass for "sake of the memories it revives." The saloon owners and white-aproned bar staff were hardly rending their garments or gnashing their teeth, as the rise in sales in whiskey and highballs meant less sugar-encrusted toddy and eggnog glasses to clean and far less time spent mixing up batches of these sometimes elaborate "Southern favorites." Part of the drop-off in sales was probably not due to any change of heart regarding the "evils" of alcohol but rather the rise in the price of eggs, milk and lemons or that the drinks were not properly displayed with a prominent position on the bar to entice patrons to develop the "$5 appetite." Another factor could have been the widely held belief at the time that sugary drinks are "injurious to the stomach" or that they cause worse hangovers than the more modern cocktails:

> *Popular ideas about drinking have changed and people do things now that they would not have considered for a moment a few years ago. For instance, there is the cocktail, which is now taken at all hours of the day, when formerly it was considered only as an appetizer. Straight whisky [sic] has the call, while the highball is growing in favor because it is less injurious to the system.*

By 1911, the apple toddy really began to fall out of favor and was generally regarded as being as "archaic as the boar's head." By the time Prohibition arrived, the toddy all but disappeared, but upon repeal, the *Baltimore Sun* declared that toddy was "legally in vogue again." It experienced a second short revival that lasted until the end of the 1940s, when changing tastes and drinkers desired something perceivably less detrimental to "the modern palate and stomach." The apple toddy would warrant a mention during the auction that sold off the spirits collection of Henry Walters, of Walters Art Gallery fame. While reminiscing with the auctioneer, Frank Wight of Sherwood Distillery recounted his family's own recipe, allegedly 150 years old:

> *You put some sugar into the bottom of a big crock and baked Baldwin apples on top of it, and then little bags containing allspice, whole cloves and a little mace all mixed up with cut up lemons. Then whiskey was poured in, sometimes as much as a gallon of it, and three-quarters as much boiling water. This was stirred vigorously for fifteen minutes and left alone for twelve days, except that it was stirred again each night and morning. Then the bags were taken out but the mixture was left marinating until Christmas. Then, of course the apples had become all soft and mushy, and a sweet delicious, spiced drink was the result. No Marylander will admit you can make this with any other liquor but rye.*

## A NOTE ON INGREDIENTS

As we stated in "The Well-Stocked Maryland Bar" section earlier in the book, you should be selective when using the modern incarnations of spirits listed in these recipes. Jamaican rum—sometimes referred to as "Jamaica spirits"—as well as Santa Cruz or St. Croix rums of the past, actually have very little to do in character with their modern counterparts. This is especially important to note when attempting to re-create the venerable Maryland apple toddy. St. Croix, most commonly represented by the brand Cruzan, is now producing rums more delicate in flavor and similar to the Cuban style. To stand up to the sugar, apples and spices, you will definitely want something more along the lines of what cocktail historian David Wondrich refers to as "pirate juice": pot-stilled, funky and full of esters.

As for the peach brandy, resist the temptation to buy the bottom-shelf bottles of sugary peach-flavored brandy; they are not the same thing. Though once common, brandy distilled from peaches can be very hard to find these days and is often prohibitively expensive for a batched drink such as the toddy. Brendan Dorr of B&O Brasserie and Cocktail Proper Consulting suggests simply substituting apple brandy instead, since the resulting change in flavor will be minimal. We've used Laird's Bottled-in-Bond Apple Brandy, as well as its Old Apple Brandy 7½ Year Old. The recently released Laird's Jersey Lightning clear apple spirit may also be fun to experiment with.

For the later recipes that call for rye whiskey, you can resort to the modern 95 percent Midwest ryes that are currently popular, but you may lose some of the subtle flavors of the toddy under all of the rye grain intensity. The obvious approach—and probably the most authentic (not to mention inexpensive!)—would be to stock up on Pikesville rye. Ordering a case from your friendly neighborhood liquor store will probably only put you back a little over $100 and will provide you with the base for many of the drinks that follow throughout the book.

# CHAPTER 4

# EGGNOG

Modern eggnog is believed to have descended from a late medieval drink called the posset, a rich mixture of heated milk, alcohol and various spices. In composition, eggnog bears many similarities to ice cream and is essentially just a dairy-and-egg mixture called a "stirred custard." In the English colonies, with the increased availability of milk, eggs and rum, eggnog gained popularity. In 1800, Issac Weld Jr. made some observations on eggnog during his travels throughout North America during the 1790s: "The American travellers [*sic*], before they pursued their journey, took a hearty draught each, according to custom, of egg-nog [*sic*], a mixture composed of new milk, eggs, rum, and sugar, beat up together."

The spirit(s) of choice for eggnog were largely demarcated along economic and geographical lines: the rich and/or those living in port cities preferred brandy, rum or some form of fortified wine. Poorer individuals or those living along frontier areas were forced to make do with whiskey, especially following the American Revolution.

In Maryland, especially in Baltimore, the eggnog and the apple toddy formed a dual-bowled, one-two punch for holiday season. No respectable household would be without the two of them gracing the sideboard, and every bar or saloon in town had them proudly perched on the back bar. Even businesses and the statehouse parties were considered incomplete without them.

We have included recipes for several historic 'nogs throughout the history of Maryland:

## EGG-NOGG

*By Mrs. Charles H. Gibson*

To make a two gallon bowl of egg-nogg [*sic*] take the yolks of thirty eggs, beat light, adding two and a half pounds of fine sugar gradually. Then pour the liquor on the eggs slowly so as to cook the eggs. Half gallon French brandy or good old whiskey, one quart Jamaica rum, one quart peach brandy; fill the bowl with rich cream. Beat some of the whites very stiff with sugar, putting it over the top of the bowl. Grate some nutmeg over the whole.

Edgar Allan Poe, as depicted by William Sartain. *Library of Congress.*

## POE FAMILY EGGNOG

*Adapted from* A Second Helping of Murder

7 eggs, separated
1 cup sugar
5 cups whole milk, divided
½ cup heavy whipping cream
1½ cups brandy
¼ cup rum
nutmeg

1. In a medium bowl, combine egg yolks and sugar, whisking until thick and pale. Set aside.
2. Fill a large bowl with ice water and set aside. In a small saucepan, warm 3 cups milk over low heat. Whisk 1 cup warm milk into yolk mixture. Add this back to the milk in the pan, stirring over low heat until combined and thickened. Remove from heat and quickly stir in cream.

3. Place saucepan in prepared ice bath. Stir occasionally until chilled, then add brandy, rum, and remaining 2 cups milk.

4. Pour eggnog into glasses. In a medium bowl with a handheld mixer, beat egg whites until soft peaks form. Spoon egg whites over eggnog, and top with grated nutmeg.

—⟨∅∅⟩—

## BALTIMORE EGGNOG

*A typical "port city" eggnog, this Baltimore version uses a mixture of cognac, dark rum and Madeira. Simon Difford, of* Class Magazine *and* Difford's Guide *fame, describes this classic as "a rich meal of a drink with a whole egg and cream—fortified with cognac, rum and Madeira."*

1 ounce cognac
1 ounce dark rum
½ ounce Madeira
1 whole egg
½ ounce simple syrup
½ ounce heavy cream
½ ounce milk

Vigorously shake all ingredients with ice and fine strain into a chilled glass. Dust with freshly grated nutmeg.

—⟨∅∅⟩—

## FRANKLIN FARMS EGGNOG

*Recipe adapted from John Phillip Hill, Franklin Farms, Baltimore*

1 egg, separated
1 wine glass cream
1 wine glass spirits
1 tablespoonful of sugar
spirits: 1/3 peach brandy, 2/3 Jamaica rum, or all rye whiskey

The yolk of the egg should be beaten hard and long, separately. The cream is then slowly poured and stirred in and the spirits then added in a thin stream, the mass meanwhile being stirred.

Half of the beaten whites are then stirred in, and the other half of the whites are beaten and poured on top. To make two gallons, use 2 dozen eggs, 4 quarts cream, 3 pints spirits and 1 pound sugar.

## CHAPTER 5

# THE RISE OF THE INN AND TAVERN

I n 1661, almost thirty years after the initial settlement of the colony, Lord Baltimore reported no alehouses or taverns present in Maryland. By the end of the seventeenth century, not only were taverns a thriving business, but they were also self-sufficiently producing enough of their own alcohol to

Old Tavern, Piscataway, Prince George's County, Maryland. Historic American Buildings Survey. Delos H Smith and John O. Brostrup, photographers. *Library of Congress.*

Reynold's Tavern, Annapolis, Maryland. E.H. Pickering, photographer. *Library of Congress.*

Blue Ball Tavern established circa 1710, Cecil County, Maryland. Historic American Buildings Survey. E.H. Pickering, photographer. *Library of Congress.*

serve their patrons. As it did in the other English colonies on the American eastern seaboard, the tavern or inn served many roles in the society of colonial Maryland. In addition to the obvious function of serving travelers as they stopped for food and drink, the tavern doubled as a circuit court for traveling judges and served as the social center of the community where townspeople could stay informed about the latest news and gossip.

Despite the slow growth of tavern culture in Maryland, the first Baltimore City Directory listed ninety-eight taverns and inns by 1796. Though most of these establishments near the waterfront were little more than crude lodgings for the droves of sailors who flooded the port city, the area west of Jones Falls was filled with such evocatively named haunts as the Golden Horse, the White Swan, the Golden Lamb, the Black Bear and the Maypole. The same was to be seen to the east in Old Town, where the likes of the Bulls Head and the Rising Sun welcomed the road-worn traveler. Indeed, at nearly every point where a popularly traveled highway entered the town, there was a tavern or English-style inn.

## INDIAN QUEEN HOTEL

One of the earliest known hotels in the city was Amos Fogg's Indian Queen Hotel, formerly located on the southwest corner of Baltimore (then Market) and Hanover Streets. Contemporary accounts state that the Indian Queen's cooks "served food that pleased even the French" and that guests were given slippers whilst their shoes or boots received complimentary polishing overnight. It was here that Francis Scott Key worked on his revised draft of "The Star-Spangled Banner" after his release from the British in September 1814.

## FOUNTAIN INN

*Mr. Grant opened an inn and tavern at the Sign of the Fountain for the accommodation of Gentlemen, their servants, and horses in the best manner.*
—Maryland Journal and Baltimore Advertiser

Opening in 1773, the Fountain Inn once stood at the southwestern corner of what is now Baltimore and Hanover Streets. Constructed in "the old

London style," it featured balconies that looked out on a tree-shaded central courtyard. The Fountain Inn was first managed by a Philadelphian, late of the Indian Queen Hotel, named Daniel Grant and would soon become the most popular inn in Baltimore.

In 1775, the inn played host to General Washington as he was on his way to meet with the Continental Congress. He stopped here again in 1781 while he was en route to Yorktown and once again in 1783 on his trip to resign his commission in Annapolis. His wife, Martha, often frequented the Fountain Inn, stopping off now and again while on her way to join the general in encampment. In fact, during the war, the inn proved to be a popular headquarters for the Patriots: the Whig Society used it to keep a watch on potential Tory loyalists, and the Council of Safety used it to hold its meetings. General Nathanael Greene also paid a visit to the Fountain Inn when he was honored at a public dinner to celebrate his victories in the southern theater of the war.

The Fountain Inn weathered the War of 1812 with its popularity intact and would host a victory dinner for Commodore Oliver Hazard Perry after his success at the Battle of Lake Erie. Even President James Madison was there, having driven all the way from Washington to be present for the festivities. Subsequent honors would be held for General Winfield Scott and Maryland-born commodore Stephen Decatur.

In 1824, the now aging Marquis de Lafayette was afforded a suite of rooms at the Fountain Inn while on a tour of America forty-three years after his initial arrival in the country.

As the years wore on, the inn's popularity waned, though its proximity to the basin of the Chesapeake made it a continual favorite of Eastern Shore and southern Maryland planters arriving into the city by boat. Daniel Grant was eventually succeeded by John H. Barney, and the inn eventually changed its name to the Fountain Hotel.

# CHAPTER 6

# MARYLAND RYE

*Three drinks of rye whiskey would double the pleasure to be got out of*
Il Trovatore. *Try it yourself.*
—H.L. Mencken

From the end of the Civil War to the onset of Prohibition, Maryland was synonymous with rye whiskey. On a national production scale, Maryland ranked third overall, only surpassed by the much larger states of fellow rye giant Pennsylvania and the birthplace of bourbon, Kentucky.

Prior to the rise of rye whiskey, rum, primarily from distilleries in Massachusetts and Rhode Island, was the hard spirit of choice for the average Maryland colonist. Although rum was arguably the first American spirit, the rise of taxation by the British government and eventual blockade by the Royal Navy brought trade between the thirteen colonies and the Caribbean islands to a halt and, with it, the materials required to produce the molasses-based spirit.

The history of American whiskey begins with western Maryland and Pennsylvania, which enjoy the shared geology of an underlying limestone shield that brought with it the bonus of water soft enough to tame the sometimes fiery nature of the original native spirit. In the years since the founding, Maryland's tobacco economy had taken its toll on the farmland, depleting it of much-needed nutrients and nitrogen. Rye, chosen as a suitable cover crop, was shown to restore those nitrates and was well known to German settlers, having been the primary bread grain of their original homeland. Surplus grain soon fell into

A 1903 Melvale Rye advertisement included in *Bones, Molars, and Briefs*, an annual publication of the University of Maryland School of Medicine. *Archive.org.*

the hands of Ulster-Irish settlers in Maryland's western counties, who brought with them their ancestral knowledge of distillation.

The rye whiskey of the late eighteenth century, farm distilled in crude pot stills and aged briefly in rough-hewn barrels, bore a scant resemblance to the 95 percent rye barrel aged in Midwest warehouses that we primarily encounter today. Far more lucrative than trading in grain, a barrel of whiskey was far easier to transport and more cost effective mile to pound than either grain or flour. The demand was so great that even the Continental army records show large purchases of rye whiskey for both medicinal and morale purposes. General Washington himself was known to have a still or two firing on the grounds of Mount Vernon.

## WHISKEY REBELLION

Following the revolution, the fledgling federal government was faced with the herculean task of recouping the enormous debt racked up during the war. As one of its first acts, the government rolled out a plan concocted by then secretary of the treasury Alexander Hamilton that would tax the distillation of "spirituous liquors." Not surprisingly, three out of four of Maryland's congressmen voted against the measure.

The resultant backlash against the tax should have been foreseen, for not only did it tax the actual whiskey produced but also the capacity of a still should it be idle. It also required cash payment, which added a further hardship to the settlers on Maryland's western outreaches, who were cash-poor and still dependent on the traditional barter system for their everyday needs.

By 1794, most of the uprisings were put down by a federal militia larger in total manpower than that used to fight the recent war of independence. Noncompliance and violent demonstrations were largely confined to western Pennsylvania, but Maryland saw its share of minor disturbances clustered around Cumberland, Hagerstown and Middletown. There was also a fear in Frederick that the "Whiskey Boys" would come and empty the state arsenal of its weapons. In the end, the Maryland rye producers would be two-time losers, as many of the tax resisters would evacuate down the Ohio River to Kentucky and, once there, develop Bourbon whiskey, which would ultimately unseat rye as the national spirit of choice.

## THE NINETEENTH CENTURY

By 1796, Baltimore's first census listed no fewer than four full-scale commercial distilleries. One of the earliest was the Joseph White Distillery, a "green" operation. It was said that the distillery's spent mash, the grain used up during the initial fermentation process, went to local farmers as free hog feed.

Once Thomas Jefferson was in office in 1802, the whiskey tax was reduced to minimal levels, and from 1810 to 1840, the number of distilleries in America doubled. The resultant boom ushered in the nation's highest levels of liquor consumption in its short history. Though the sheer number of individual distilleries would fall off in the following years, the capacity per site continued to rise.

Prior to the spread of saloon culture, local grocers were the primary dispensers of Maryland's liquor and whiskey, supplied by local farms and taverns and their hundreds of small stills. Even the famous Johns Hopkins, a Quaker by faith, sold whiskey under the brand name Hopkins Best out of his Hopkins Brothers grocery, a fact that would later get him thrown out of a Friends meeting.

# THE WALTERS

Born in 1819 in the central Pennsylvania town of Liverpool, William Thompson Walters came to Baltimore in the 1840s. Starting off in the grain business, by 1847 Walters had established a wholesale liquor business and was importing whiskey from four different Pennsylvania distillers. Soon, Walters was at the helm of one of the largest whiskey operations in the area and soon took up residence in the fashionable Mount Vernon Place district in Baltimore.

At the outbreak of the American Civil War, Walters—who had been an outspoken proponent of states' rights to leave the union—left with his family to tour Europe in an effort to both study and purchase works of art. In 1882, William disbanded his operation, and Edwin, his younger brother, went into business for himself, purchasing the old Maitland & Bryan's Distillery in Canton and rechristening it Orient Distillers. The new operation was large enough to warrant its own dock, and soon Orient Pure Rye was available nationwide.

A portrait of William T. Walters, by artist Paul Adolphe Rajon. *Walters Art Gallery, via Wikimedia Commons.*

A nineteenth-century ad for W.T. Walters and Company. *Archive.org.*

## NEEDWOOD DISTILLERY

It was also during this time that rye production in western Maryland took off. Washington County alone sported no fewer than twenty-six commercial grain distilleries, with most activity centered on Leitersburg just north of Hagerstown. The largest distillery prior to the 1860s was run by Robert Fowler and Frederick K. Zeigler. Located on Antietam Creek, it boasted a twenty-horsepower engine and could process fifty to sixty bushels of grain in one day.

Around the same time that the Walters were getting underway, Outerbridge Horsey II, namesake of his father, the former U.S. senator from Delaware, set up a commercial distillery between Burkittsville and Brunswick, in Frederick County, and utilized the waters from the nearby Catoctin Mountains. Horsey would suffer a major setback during the Civil War when marauding troops from both sides of the Mason-Dixon left the distillery in a state of ruin.

Horsey, who was luckily out of the States at the time, took the misfortune as an opportunity to study the distilling techniques and equipment of major European and Scottish distilleries and, upon his return home in 1865, rebuilt and completely modernized Needwood into a seven-acre plant with a warehouse that could hold up to three thousand whiskey barrels. Needwood even began to import some Irish grain and, under supervisor James Dall, began to manufacture a deliberately upmarket new 100-proof rye whiskey under the brand name Horsey's Pure Rye. At the time, there was a belief that time spent traveling inside the barrel was superior to simple warehousing, so each batch of whiskey was shipped by sea around Cape Horn to San Francisco and then shipped back to Maryland via rail.

## LANAHAN AND STEWART

In 1855, Lanahan and Stewart began production of Hunter Pure Rye, later known as Hunter Baltimore Rye, a brand name that would last well into the repeal era following national Prohibition.

Stewart Pure Rye bottles. *Authors' photo*.

## CIVIL WAR

By the dawn of the 1860s, Maryland rye was in vogue and in high demand, but wartime always proved disastrous for the Maryland rye industry, and the Civil War was no exception. In both the run up to the conflict and during Reconstruction, the liquor tax rate skyrocketed. Initially, rye sales boomed, as veterans from both sides of the battles in Maryland had developed a taste for the local whiskey and the wartime improvements to the U.S. railways allowed firms to satisfy the demand. However, this improvement would ultimately cause great harm to the industry overall, as cheaper, out-of-state brands were now easier to ship into Maryland.

Despite the hostile business environment, new brands such as Pen-Mar, Indian Springs and Kemp Mill sprang up. As problems arose in the growing of rye in state (there were some accounts of a wild onion infestation), Maryland firms were tempted to ship in rye from areas such as New York or Wisconsin.

New labels from Pennsylvania's Monongahela region began to pour in, and Maryland soon fell under the "imported is better than domestic"

W.T. Walters and Company advertisement from the auction guide to Henry Walters's liquor collection. *Authors' collection.*

mindset. The out-of-state brands gained a premium product reputation. This misconception was helped along to a great extent by William Walters and his partner, Charles Harvey, who along with some firms began misleadingly adding "Monongahela" to their Maryland rye whiskey labels, hoping that an uninformed public wouldn't actually know anything about geography.

## SHERWOOD DISTILLING

In 1868, Edward Hyatt bought out and enlarged a distillery in the Cockeysville area of Baltimore County started by grocers John J. Wight and William Lentz. Hyatt, who previously owned a whiskey dealership on Water Street with Nicholas Griffith, spent time in New York amassing start-up capital and investors before returning to Baltimore to begin Sherwood. A scarce ten years later, the U.S. Army itself was buying up Sherwood Rye to stockpile for hospital use.

In 1894, Edward Hyatt died, and John Hyatt Wight took over the company, beginning a line of Wights in Maryland whiskey production that would continue until the death of John Hyatt Wight II in 1990.

Sherwood Rye bottle from the personal collection of Henry Walters. *Authors' photo.*

# CHAPTER 7

# FIGHTING MEN, FIGHTING SHIPS AND THEIR DRINKS

## COMMODORE JOHN RODGERS (1772–1838)

*I will be glad to let you have my receipts as you request although no one to whom I have given them has taken the trouble to follow them.*
*—Commodore Rodgers*

Harford County resident and hero of the War of 1812, Commodore John Rodgers was the head of what would eventually become one of the great navy families in the country. The son of a Revolutionary War veteran, Rodgers developed an early desire to go to sea while watching vessels docked in nearby Havre de Grace. Eventually, his father relented, and after his apprenticeship, Rodgers received his first command on a merchant vessel named *Jane*, on which he performed admirably. Rodgers's service spanned the Quasi-War with France, the Barbary Wars and the War of 1812, in which he saw a great deal of action, especially during the recapture of Washington and the defense of Fort McHenry. During the war, his hometown of Havre de Grace was sacked by the forces of the infamous British admiral George Cockburn. Rodgers's own family was forced to flee their home during the attack.

Though not a huge imbiber of "spirituous drink" due to a promise made to his father at the start of his career, one of Rodgers's punch recipes survives via the family's records from their hereditary home, Sion Hill:

Sion Hill, 2026 Level Road, Havre de Grace, Harford County, Maryland. Historic American Buildings Survey. E.H. Pickering, photographer. *Library of Congress.*

## A FINE BODIED PUNCH

*Commodore John Rodgers's receipt, Sion Hill Papers, Harford County. Adapted from* Maryland's Way: The Hammond-Harwood House Cook Book.

juice of 10 lemons
1 bottle rum
1 bottle brandy
1 bottle port wine
1 bottle strong tea (but white wine is better)
½ pint curacao
3 cups pulverized white sugar

Take the rind of squeezed lemons and add them to the stock. Stir well. Let stand for a couple of hours, strain and bottle stock. (Should you use tea, it should not draw long enough to become bitter.)

By a bottle, it is understood an ordinary wine bottle, 4½ to a gallon. When punch is needed, take 8 bottles of stock with plenty

**83**

of ice. Stir well and serve. Will serve 25 to 30 persons. The stock may be allowed to settle and then filtered. This gives a good color but ordinarily is unnecessary.

# THE NAVY ACADEMY YEARS

In 1845, Secretary of the Navy George Bancroft established the United States Naval Academy (then merely referred to as the Naval School) on a three-hundred-acre campus on the former site of Fort Severn in Anne Arundel County. Three years earlier, in what would come to be known as the "Somer's Affair," the son of the secretary of war attempted to seize the vessel he was serving on and turn it to piracy. The fact that a midshipman in the United States Navy would even consider mutiny put such a fear into the top brass that they ordered the creation of

Commodore Matthew Perry. Mathew B. Brady, photographer. *Library of Congress.*

the academy so officer recruits could be properly educated and supervised in a uniform manner as opposed to the on-ship training system in place at the time. Commodore Matthew Perry, a strong advocate for the modernization of the navy, fully supported the plan and even helped to develop its new curriculum. Baltimore native commander Franklin Buchanan was chosen to be the first superintendent of the new academy.

Buchanan resigned his post in 1947 to serve in the Mexican-American War (April 25, 1846–February 2, 1848). After the war, Buchanan commanded the steam frigate *Susquehanna*, which became Perry's flagship during the commodore's expedition to Japan during the 1850s, and Buchanan was commissioned captain in 1855. Prior to the Civil War, Buchanan

Commodore Franklin Buchanan, officer of the Confederate navy. Brady National Photographic Art Gallery. *Library of Congress.*

was given command of the Washington Navy Yard, but in 1861, he resigned his commission and joined the Confederacy. Buchanan held the belief that his home state of Maryland was going to secede from the Union, but that reality never unfolded, and he pleaded to be reinstated. The secretary of the navy denied his request, stating that he had no room "halfhearted patriots."

Though mistrusted at first by his new compatriots, Buchanan had an ally in Stephen Mallory, the Confederate secretary of the navy. Mallory, who held great respect for Buchanan, heard of his reputation as one of the top commanders of the day and knew he needed the best man available to command the Confederacy's new experimental wonder-weapon: the CSS *Virginia*. Built on the unfinished hull of the former USS *Merrimack*, the ironclad *Virginia* was highly sought after as a command, and due to the seniority system in place, Buchanan had little chance of winning the captain's chair. Maneuvering around the politics, Mallory named Buchanan as the flag officer of the James River Squadron. Naturally, Buchanan chose the *Virginia* as his flagship and, because it never actually had a captain assigned, took direct command of the ironclad.

The first trip of the *Virginia* was also its first combat experience at the Battle of Hampton Roads. Boldly throwing all caution to the wind, Buchanan put the vessel's armor to the test and sailed across the broadsides of the most heavily armed ships the U.S. Navy had to offer. He rammed into the USS *Cumberland* and then turned the ship to engage the USS *Congress*. Four Union vessels moved to assist their endangered comrades, but three quickly turned back and the remaining one ran aground. The *Congress*, trying to escape the fate of the *Cumberland*, deliberately drove itself ashore to prevent sinking. The *Virginia*, impregnable by contrast, pounded the *Congress* into submission with cannon fire, forcing it to surrender.

After the surrender, Buchanan ordered his crew to rescue any wounded and secure the *Congress*'s officers as prisoners. The rest of the Union sailors were allowed to make the relatively easy swim to shore. As they were in enemy territory with no hope of towing the *Congress* back as a prize, Buchanan gave the order to set the defeated ship ablaze. While undergoing the rescue operation, Union troops from the shore opened fire, killing several men from both sides. Furious, Buchanan took to the *Virginia*'s top deck and returned fire with his own musket until a Minié ball struck him in the thigh, nearly striking the femoral artery. Wounded and unable to continue command, Buchanan ordered the crew to destroy the *Congress* with hot shot and for his executive officer to assume command for what would be the fateful battle with the Union ironclad *Monitor* the following day.

After his recovery, Buchanan was promoted to the rank of admiral—the first for the Confederacy—and sent to Mobile Bay to command the Confederate fleet against Union rear admiral David Farragut. On August 5, 1864, the fight did not go in Buchanan's favor, and he was wounded in the leg again while aboard the USS *Tennessee* and taken prisoner. He was released during a prisoner exchange in February 1865 and spent the rest of the war recovering, as this injury resulted in the amputation of his leg.

The recipe that follows is reportedly a personal recipe from Buchanan and is in the style of the "clarified milk punch" of the late seventeenth century

*Merrimac and Monitor.* From *Young Folks History of the War for the Union* (1881), by John Denison Champlin. *Archive.org.*

in which milk is intentionally curdled with the addition of citrus and the solids strained out. The process may sound revolting, but punches of the same style have been described as "something so smooth and luxurious as to be absolutely perilous." This process also helps the drink to take on a beautiful amber color. The recipe bears many similarities to the "India Milk Punch" that crops up in contemporary cookbooks. The name is probably a reference to Buchanan's trip through Egypt while en route to Japan during Perry's voyage; otherwise there is nothing particularly "Egyptian" about it.

———⋙⋘———

## ADMIRAL FRANKLIN BUCHANAN'S FAMOUS EGYPTIAN PUNCH

*Recipe by Amelia Pinkney D. Lurman, Harford County Maryland. Adapted from* Maryland's Way: The Hammond-Harwood House Cook Book.

18 lemons
4 pounds white sugar
5 quarts boiled water
2 whole nutmegs, grated
2 quarts boiled milk

2½ quarts good brandy
2½ quarts Jamaica rum

Peel lemons and steep in 1 quart rum for twenty-four hours, covering closely. Next day, squeeze lemon juice over sugar. Pour boiling water over the rinds. Let stand until cool and then squeeze and remove rinds. Add grated nutmeg, water and scalded [boiled] milk. Stir all ingredients together for at least ten minutes. Add brandy and rum. Stir. Strain through cheesecloth into a jar or crock, then clear through filter paper. It will drip through as a clear amber color. Serve shilled over cracked ice. If kept in a warm place while filtering, it will drip faster. This makes about 14 quarts. Treasured family receipt.

# ADMIRAL TIMOTHY J. KELEHER

Rear Admiral Timothy J Keleher was a 1908 Naval Academy graduate. In 1938, he was named the director of the marine engineering department. The admiral and his wife, Eugenia, were fixtures in Annapolis party circles during his tenure with the academy. After retirement, he served on the board of trustees for the Naval Academy Alumni Association. Fortunately, several of the couple's house recipes are preserved in the 1964 edition of *Maryland's Way* by the Hammond-Harwood House Association, including this one for punch:

## ARMY AND NAVY PUNCH

*Recipe by Admiral Timothy J. Keleher, Annapolis, Maryland. Adapted from*
Maryland's Way: The Hammond-Harwood House Cook Book.

1 gallon French brandy
1 quart Jamaican rum
1 quart peach brandy
1 pint curacao
Juice of 2 dozen lemons
1¼ pounds fine granulated sugar

Dress with small slices of orange and lemon. When ready to serve put in a lump of ice. Will serve 25 people. Strong but good.

# PART III

~•/•/•~

# THE GOLDEN AGE

## 1860–1919

Though often debated, the Golden Age of the American cocktail began sometime in the mid- to late nineteenth century and was cut short by the onset of national Prohibition. During this short span, we see the greatest period of development in the art of the American bar ever, and the number of classic drinks created at this time are too numerous to list.

A street view of Baltimore in 1912. *Library of Congress.*

## COCKTAIL TIMELINE

1862: Jerry Thomas publishes *The Bar-Tender's Guide*, the first cocktail book.

1867: Rose's Lime Juice is patented by Lauchlin Rose.

1882: Harry Johnson publishes *The Bartenders Manual*.

1888: The Ramos Gin Fizz is invented at the Imperial Cabinet Saloon in New Orleans by Henry Ramos.

1895: Patrick Gavin Duffy invents the highball.

1896: The Marguerite Cocktail, one of the most likely ancestors to the martini, appears in print.

## MARYLAND COCKTAIL TIMELINE

1861: The first bloodshed of the Civil War occurs in Baltimore.

1862: Confederate forces are defeated at Antietam. Remembered as the "Single Bloodiest Day of the Civil War," the Battle of Antietam takes place in Sharpsburg, with casualties numbering more than twenty-three thousand.

1864: Maryland abolishes slavery.

1865: President Abraham Lincoln is assassinated by John Wilkes Booth. Abbott's Bitters is founded in Baltimore in this year.

1869: Barnum's Hotel at the corner of Calvert and Fayette Streets (dubbed the best hotel in the United States by Charles Dickens) holds a dinner for the seventeenth U.S. president, Andrew Johnson, that features ninety items of Maryland cuisine, from elk to turtle.

1876: Johns Hopkins University is founded.

1886: The Enoch Pratt Free Library opens in Baltimore.

1895: George Herman "Babe" Ruth is born in Baltimore, near the present-day site of Oriole Park at Camden Yards.

1904: At 2:00 a.m. on February 8, thirty-five Western Union telegraph operators start tapping out news of the Great Baltimore Fire from the House of Welsh restaurant, on whose corner of Guilford and Saratoga the last remaining telegraph pole that carried lines in every direction stood. For three days, the operators send out news from the restaurant.

1906: The Frozen Rye is created.

1909: The Frozen Rye is mentioned in the *Baltimore Sun*. The Art Gallery building, constructed by financier and philanthropist Henry Walters

(1848–1931), opens at the northwest corner of North Charles and East Centre Streets, facing the south square of Washington Place.

1914: A Frozen Rye recipe appears in *Beverages de Luxe*, attributed to the Belvedere Hotel in Baltimore. The Hippodrome Theatre is built on Eutaw Street between West Fayette and Redwood Streets and shows early silent movies and burlesque live shows. The Baltimore Museum of Art is founded and opens at the old mansion that once belonged to Mary Elizabeth Garrett.

1917: Lithuanian Hall opens in East Baltimore.

# CHAPTER 8

# BALTIMORE'S GRAND HOTEL BARS

By the 1820s, fashions changed, and these Old World–style institutions were slowly torn down to be replaced by newer, more elaborate hotels.

## BARNUM'S CITY HOTEL

*The most comfortable of all the hotels of which I had an experience in the United States and they were not a few, is Barnum's, in that city (Baltimore); where the English traveler will find curtains to his bed for the first and probably last time in America…and where he will likely to have enough water for washing himself, which is not at all a common case.*
*—Charles Dickens, 1842*

In 1825, an investor group led by David Barnum began construction of a new hotel, at the southwest corner of Fayette and Calvert Streets, nestled among the fashionable Georgian dwellings on Monument Square. Clocking in at seven stories, the new venture flaunted Baltimore's newfound status and sheer capitalist wealth as the second-largest city of the time, with its columns and steps and upper-floor windows sporting elegant wrought-iron balconies. Inside, visitors were greeted with lush red velvet curtains and colossal glass mirrors that stretched from the plush carpeted floors to the ceiling in great, gilded baroque frames.

*Left*: Charles Dickens. Eliphalet M. Brown, lithographer. *Library of Congress.*

*Right*: Washington Irving. Jas S. King, engraver. *Library of Congress.*

Barnum cut his teeth in the hotel industry with an apprenticeship at the venerable Indian Queen Hotel years earlier and would serve as his namesake hotel's manager until his death in 1844 at age seventy-four.

The Barnum has the distinction of hosting famed British writer Charles Dickens during his first American tour in 1842. Normally very critical of his accommodations in the States, Dickens seemed to have nothing but nice things to say about the rooms at Barnum's. It was also the site of his first mint julep, sent over by the nearby Guy's Monument Hotel. Apparently it was such a large bowl (juleps were often served punch-style at the time) that Dickens invited his American friend Washington Irving over to help him finish it.

Here is Dickens's own recollection of the event:

> *Some unknown admirer of his* [Irving] *books and mine sent to the hotel a most enormous mint julep, wreathed with flowers. We sat, one on either side of it, with great solemnity (it filled a respectably-sized round table), but the solemnity was of very short duration. It was quite an enchanted julep, and carried us among innumerable people and places that we both knew. The*

*julep held out far into the night, and my memory never saw him afterwards otherwise than as bending over it, with his straw, with an attempted air of gravity (after some anecdote involving some wonderfully droll and delicate observation of character), and then as his eye caught mine, melting into that captivating laugh of his, which was the brightest and best I have ever heard.*

## MINT JULEP

Unbeknownst to many people, Maryland was once part of the "julep belt" that stretched from here through Virginia and Georgia all the way to Kentucky. Regional preferences would prevail, and there are far too many controversial issues with this drink to cover in this small format. Here is a Maryland mint julep recipe, made with the mandatory rye whiskey, from Frederic Arnold Kummer of Baltimore:

*Crush one lump of sugar at the bottom of a tall glass. Add half a dozen small sprigs of mint, which should first be lightly twisted between the fingers to break the skin of the leaves. Cover with whiskey and allow to stand for ten minutes. Then pour in balance of whiskey (to make a long drink a full whiskey glass should be used), fill the glass with finely crushed ice and stir rapidly with a spoon until the outside of the glass is frosted. Serve garnished with mint sprigs. The best Maryland juleps were made with old rye.*

A much-later recipe appears in the 1941 edition of *Here's How* by W.C. Whitfield. Described as "The Maryland Compromise," it calls for a gentle bruising of the mint.

## MARYLAND MINT JULEP

1½ teaspoons powdered sugar. Dissolve this in water.
4 sprigs fresh mint. Bruise, but do not crush.
2 jiggers rye whiskey

Put these in a tall glass filled with crushed ice, stir until frosted and decorate with more mint.

## RENNERT HOTEL

In 1885, at the southwest corner of what is now Liberty and Saratoga Streets, hotelier Robert Rennert built the new flagship hotel of his empire. Dubbed the "Palace of the South," the Rennert Hotel, a towering mass of brick and brownstone designed by E.F. Baldwin, was an overnight success.

Almost from the start, the Rennert was nationally renowned by the political set, who flocked to what was then considered "the best restaurant in America." There, an all-black staff masterfully crafted such regional delicacies as diamondback terrapin—kept live in basement cages before serving—local game birds and the ever-popular Maryland beaten biscuits. Another draw was the raw oyster bar, a luxury that was only just beginning to appear in the finest establishments. Baltimore writer H.L. Mencken was a frequent guest and could often be found in the Rennert's main dining room, mingling among a who's who of the Baltimore elite.

The hotel's fortunes slumped with the passage of national Prohibition in 1919, and the owners soon fell behind on their taxes. The Rennert, so

The Rennert Hotel. *Authors' collection.*

*Left*: Diamondback Lounge logo. *Authors' collection.*

*Below*: Jane Grant Howard's Maryland Apple Toddy. *Authors' photo.*

Peggy Stewart Tea Punch. *Authors' photo.*

Maryland Mint Julep. *Authors' photo.*

Frozen Rye à la Belvedere.
*Authors' photo.*

Farmer's Bishop. *Authors' photo.*

*Left*: The Belvedere. *Photo courtesy of Keith and Jessica Hawks.*

*Below*: The Diamondback. *Photo courtesy of Keith and Jessica Hawks.*

The Preakness. *Authors' photo.*

Admiral Keleher's Army and Navy Punch. *Authors' photo.*

*Left*: Keith Hipsley, champion home brewer of Lithuanian extraction, adds rye whiskey to a batch of virytas. *Authors' photo.*

*Below*: A completed batch of Lithuanian virytas. *Authors' photo.*

*Right*: Bar tools. *Authors' photo.*

*Below*: Brendan Dorr, head bartender of B&O American Brasserie. *Authors' photo.*

*Left*: Aaron Joseph, lead bartender at Wit & Wisdom. *Authors' photo.*

*Below*: Brendan Dorr's Line State Punch. *Authors' photo.*

The Farragut Cocktail
by Aaron Joseph at Wit
& Wisdom. *Authors' photo.*

Aaron Joseph's Papa Na
Pua. *Authors' photo.*

*Left*: An original creation by Melissa Ray of the Owl Bar, Belvedere. *Authors' photo.*

*Below*: The John Eager Howard Room at the Belvedere. *Photo courtesy of the Belvedere.*

Lyon Distilling's rye whiskey. *Photo courtesy of Jaime Windon.*

Lyon Distilling's product line. *Photo courtesy of Jaime Windon.*

*Left*: The distilling process. *Photo courtesy of Jaime Windon.*

*Below*: Sloop Betty Vodka. *Photo courtesy of Blackwater Distilling.*

Picaroon Rum. *Photo courtesy of Blackwater Distilling.*

Millstone Cidery. *Authors' photo.*

Millstone Cidery's Farmgate Cider. *Authors' photo.*

Millstone Cidery's main building in Monkton, Maryland. *Authors' photo.*

Cider barrels.
*Authors' photo.*

Cider settlings.
*Authors' photo.*

*Above*: Jon Blair puts the finishing touches on a glass of Tom and Jerry at the Forgotten Cocktail Club. *Authors' photo.*

*Left*: Lyon Distilling's still. *Photo courtesy of Jaime Windon.*

far into the red, fell into receivership at the close of the Great Depression. When Prohibition was repealed in 1933 and H.L. Mencken celebrated "liberty restored" with Baltimore's first legal beer at the Rennert's bar, there was some optimism that the hotel could regain some of its lost glory, but time and neglect had taken its toll on the almost fifty-year-old structure. The Rennert's fate was sealed in 1934, when the ceiling of its main dining room collapsed on the drunken revelers at a fraternity dance. The Rennert shuttered five years later and was demolished to make way for a parking garage in 1941.

## THE BELVEDERE HOTEL: A COCKTAIL TIME CAPSULE

*Since proper Edwardian ladies abhorred drinking and cigar smoke, my Bar Room was pretty much off limits to the fairer sex when I first opened. This was a man's environment with rough talk, spittoons and bookmakers. No, the ladies did not wish to be present and those gentlemen really didn't want them there.*
*Rows of sparkling glasses were carefully stacked along the back bar mirror as well as hundreds of bottles of all shapes and sizes with colorful labels advertising the intoxicating elixirs they contained.*
*The regulars would start gathering around four in the afternoon calling out loudly to each other and gathering in groups along the stand-up bar or around the tables.*
*Huge frosty mugs of local draft beer would come sliding along the bar quenching the thirst of many a parched socialite. Others preferred Maryland Rye or shot glasses of amber bourbon or whiskey. The more they drank, the louder the discussions became and sometimes arguments had to be settled with a good old fashioned fisticuffs, blue-bloods or not!*
*—Colonel Consolvo, owner of the Belvedere, 1917–36*

The Belvedere Hotel opened on December 14, 1903, in the upscale neighborhood of Mt. Vernon at the corner of Charles and Chase Streets. Designed in the Beaux-Arts style, it was named for Belvidere, the former residence of Revolutionary War general John Eager Howard. With four hundred rooms, it was at the time of its opening Baltimore's premier hotel and one of the most impressive that the city had yet seen. The hotel was the site of the Duke of Windsor's bachelor party— his fiancée, Wallis Simpson, and her friends decided on a night out at the theater.

The Belvedere Hotel. *Authors' collection.*

The 1912 Democratic Convention outside the Belvedere Hotel. *Library of Congress.*

In its latter years, the Belvedere became the traditional host for out-of-town teams playing against the Baltimore Orioles. During one stay, Mickey Mantle was arrested for public drunkenness.

When it opened, the impressive bar room—complete with Teutonic herringbone brick walls, leaded stained-glass windows and imposing dark wooden benches—was yet unnamed and was simply referred to as the "bar at the Belvedere." It is unclear when the signature duo of blinking, amber-eyed owls that eventually lent their name to the bar actually appeared, but legend has it that Colonel Consolvo, the owner of the hotel during the Prohibition era, placed them there to signal patrons that whiskey—hidden away in the hotel basement—was available. The owls remained after Prohibition, but even by 1941, the room was still only referred to as the bar at the Belvedere. When under control of the Sheraton Corporation in the 1950s, the bar was rebranded as the Fallstaff Room, with the waitstaff appropriately dressed in ridiculous faux-Elizabethan attire, and the bar's popularity began to wane.

The hotel closed in 1971, and the owls mysteriously disappeared. Five years later, when Victor Frenkil bought the beleaguered Belvedere, he went on a frantic search for the iconic birds. The tips led all over the East Coast, resulting in some secret meetings straight out of a detective novel, but the owls were nowhere to be found. Finally, in April 1977, after extensive renovations to the bar had been completed, the wayward owls were returned in the middle of the night, bypassing both locked door and the hotel watchman, complete with a cryptic note attached to the bar door:

*Where we've been*
*What we've seen*
*No matter the din*
*No one will glean*
*But if your eyes are clear*
*Today you can tell*
*The Owls of the Belvedere*
*Have returned from Hell*

In addition to its many claims to fame, the Belvedere and the Owl Bar hold a unique significance in the history of Maryland alcohol culture in that it is the only establishment to date with a written record of its pre-Prohibition drink recipes. Recorded in 1908 (and reprinted in 1914) in *Beverages de Luxe*—a publication of the *Wine and Spirits Bulletin* out of Louisville, Kentucky—the Belvedere is afforded a full-page spread alongside such storied institutions as the Pendennis Club, the Waldorf-Astoria and the St. Charles Hotel. Signed by N. Storm, the wine steward of the time, it lists seven recipes, five of which appear to be unique to the Belvedere. Also included are the Royal Smile (simply a renamed "Jack Rose") and a modified recipe for Philadelphia's Clover Club identical to the one being served by Harry Craddock. The first cocktail included in the list, the Frozen Rye, is covered in depth in the next chapter, and the rest are included here for reference.

## MOON COCKTAIL

Distinctly Our Own
Few dashes of Grenadine Syrup.
One-sixth of Italian Vermouth.
One-sixth of French Vermouth.
Two-thirds Apple Brandy.
Stirred with spoon or shaken.
Cocktail glass.

## BELVEDERE COCKTAIL

A Good Morning Bracer.
One-third Italian Vermouth.
One-Third Gordon Gin.
One Third Irish Whiskey.
Few dashes of Absinthe.
Cocktail glass.
Well frapped.

## THE ROYAL SMILE

Juice of half a lime.
One-fourth Grenadine Syrup.
One-fourth Gordon Gin.
One-half Apple Brandy.
Cocktail glass.

## CLOVER CLUB

Juice of lime.
Few dashes of Grenadine Syrup.
One-sixth Italian Vermouth.
One-sixth French Vermouth.
Two-thirds gin.
Add white of an egg. Frappe well. Dress with three mint leaves on
edge of glass.
Serve in claret glass.
In season, use raspberries instead of Grenadine. Macerate the
raspberries with muddler.

## PERFECT COCKTAIL

One-sixth Italian Vermouth.
One sixth French Vermouth.
Two-thirds Gordon Gin.
Well frapped with a piece of orange peel.
Cocktail glass.

---

## PICK ME UP

Juice of whole orange.
Jigger of gin.
White of an egg.
Highball glass.
Well frapped.

# CHAPTER 9

# 1908: THE FROZEN RYE

In the history of Maryland cocktails, no other drink has had the sheer staying power of the Frozen Rye. Emerging from the hotel bar scene in the early 1900s, it fled overseas with American expats during Prohibition and made a brief resurgence during repeal days before going underground and ensconcing itself among the country club elite.

The Belvedere sign today. *Authors' photo.*

The first recipe we have for the Frozen Rye appears in the *Beverages de Luxe* pamphlet published in 1908. The 1914 reprint—identical to the first edition—includes the Frozen Rye in a long list of contemporary cocktails served at the Belvedere Hotel's yet-to-be-named Owl Bar. In addition to such well-known classics as the Clover Club and the Royal Smile (merely a renaming of the sometimes controversial "Jack Rose" cocktail), the Frozen Rye is listed alongside some of the hotel's other signature cocktails. A complex mix of rye whiskey, orange curacao, pineapple syrup and a selection of citrus juices, the Frozen Rye was served in a "large champagne glass" filled with "fine ice" and served with a straw. Melissa Ray, one of the head bartenders at the present-day Owl Bar, believes that the large champagne glass mentioned is similar to the balloon-shaped glass popularized by Dushan Zaric's Employees Only bar in New York City.

## THE BELVEDERE FROZEN RYE

Juice of half lime
Few dashes orange juice
Few dashes pineapple syrup
Few dashes orange Curacoa [*sic*]
Balance rye whiskey

Serve in a large champagne glass. Put slice of orange and slice of pineapple in glass, allowing same to stick out beyond top of glass. Fill same with fine ice and pour drink over same, with cherry on top. Serve with straw.

Following its publication in *Beverages de Luxe*, the Frozen Rye is mentioned by name in the October 1909 *Baltimore Sun* "The Fashion in Drinks" article. The unnamed author interviews a likewise unnamed bartender from an unknown hotel who discusses at length the difficulty a professional bartender encounters while trying to stay current with all of the emerging cocktails. "The fashion in drinks are daily changing to suit changing taste and seasons," he said. "I will tell you, it keeps us on the jump to know exactly how to mix for some of the new drinks asked for nowadays." The bartender went on to discuss popular drink trends, noting that the perennially popular Manhattan was somewhat out of favor with Baltimore palates and losing ground to the new "great favorite" the Bronx, but he said that the martini was still going as strong as ever. When asked specifically about the popularity of any new drinks, he had this to say: "There was a drink started in this town about a year ago which, I am told, is a big success in a number of cities now. It's called a frozen rye and they tell me it's an awfully smooth drink. It's one of those kinds that fool you, unless you're a connoisseur of mixed drinks."

Around the same time, the Belvedere Hotel began hosting a weekday afternoon tea and dance social. Called the *thé dansant* and featuring live music and dancing, the Belvedere hoped to appeal to Baltimore's young people and office workers who were looking for a little social interaction and entertainment after a long day's work. Contrary to the name, tea itself was rarely served, but the Frozen Rye and the famous Belvedere mint juleps were in high demand. "Just one of these ambrosial concoctions would keep a man happy until bedtime," one *Sun* writer commented.

By the time of Prohibition, when drinking in public was driven underground, the Frozen Rye made the leap across the Atlantic and surfaced briefly in 1924 during an American expatriate Christmas celebration in Paris. To capitalize on the new influx of paying customers filling up the cafés in town, the French were swift to add familiar American favorites to their menus and revived a few classic drinks sure to appeal to the thirsty crowds suffering under the forced drying of Volstead. According to accounts, "supper could be had all the way from 50 to 500 francs. Cafés catering to Americans were quick to install the almost forgotten 'Tom and Jerry' and the equally reminiscent Maryland 'frozen rye.'"

The Frozen Rye next appeared in print in 1938, when a *Baltimore Afro-American* newspaper article mentioned that the drink was expertly served by the elite mixologists at the Vilma Tavern among the historically black nightclubs on Pennsylvania Avenue. After this, the Frozen Rye appeared on menus of popular eateries around Baltimore—Haussner's on Eastern Avenue, Miller Brothers on Fayette Street, Brooklandville's the Green Spring Inn and Spauldings in Pikesville—but it was effectively out of the news media.

Sometime between 1940 and 1960, the original Frozen Rye morphed from standard cocktail size and lengthened into the tall drink served at various country clubs around the area. Andy Ervin of Andy's Bar at the Elkridge Country Club is known to serve up a seriously potent version of this drink to this day.

## NOTE ON INGREDIENTS

Try to avoid the use of the more fiery Midwestern ryes in this cocktail, as the rye content—upward of 95 percent—will completely drown out the other components of this drink. Even Catoctin Creek out of Purcellville, Virginia (a personal favorite of ours), is a bit too rye-forward for the cocktail-sized frozen rye, but it does well in the elongated version, where added flavor is necessary. We have found favorable results with the ubiquitous Pikesville Rye, along with Leopold Maryland-Style Rye. Having recently tasted Lyon Distilling's new aged Maryland rye, we believe it will work very well with this recipe too. For something a bit different, the Lyon Free State unaged rye spirit is also very pleasant to use.

For the curacao, skip the el cheapo versions common in the local liquor store, and under no circumstances should you use the blue kind. Due to the lack of authentic curacaos on the market, Grand Marnier would be the easiest fix, but Mandarine Napoleon would produce a very tasty drink as well. If you can get your hands on a bottle of Pierre Ferrand's 1849 Dry Curacao, we highly recommend it.

## WHERE TO GET THE FROZEN RYE

ELKRIDGE CLUB
6100 North Charles Street, Baltimore, MD 21212
(410) 377-9200

# CHAPTER 10

# 1913: VIRYTAS

## LITHUANIAN MARYLAND

Fleeing from cultural suppression by the Russian government, the first wave of roughly one thousand Lithuanian immigrants—the majority tailors seeking work in the city's garment industry—began to arrive in Baltimore in the early 1880s. By the mid-decade, the population had swelled enough to warrant the organization of their own parish, and in 1887, the Saint John's Beneficial Society organized 250 members in order to purchase a suitable building for its place of worship. In the end, the congregation settled in East Baltimore in a recently renovated, former synagogue on Loyd Street.

The first incarnation of the Lithuanian social club took up residence on West Barre Street, where it remained for twelve years, until the space grew too small for the growing community's needs. Between 1916 and 1917, two buildings were purchased on Hollins and Parkin Streets in Union Square, and by 1921, the new Lithuanian Hall held a month-long opening ceremony. Lithuanian Hall ("Lith Hall" to Baltimoreans) would only be referred to by the Lithuanian name *Lietuvių Namai* until almost the 1970s.

In the 1920s, the hall would play host to several gatherings and speeches by Communist Party USA members such as William Z. Foster and Juliet Stuart Poynitz. In 1929, a speech by Sol Hurwitz grew violent as an anti-communist mob sought to interrupt the proceedings and had to be dispersed by the Baltimore City Police.

By the 1930s, "Little Lithuania" covered the area of Southwest Baltimore around South Paca, West Lombard, South Green and Hollins Streets, with the population numbering somewhere between seven thousand and fifteen thousand.

Today, Lith Hall remains as popular as ever with the ethnic community, which has spread as far as Halethorpe and Arbutus. As one of the few remaining Baltimore dance halls, it has grown increasingly popular with both the Baltimore hipster element and students from the Maryland Institute College of Art who swarm the place in order to "dance to their grandparents' music" and drink their fill of large bottles of inexpensive Lithuanian beer. On any given evening, patrons may even encounter John Waters parked at the bar, as Lith Hall is one of his favorite watering holes.

# VIRYTAS

The Baltimore Lithuanians are known for arguably the most iconic, albeit secretive, spirits in the city: virytas or viryta. Commonly brewed up around the holidays, virytas (pronounced "vititus"), is a rich honey, citrus and spice liqueur and is a fixture at any Lithuanian celebration, be it at Lith Hall, the VFW or in a private home. As the saying goes, "It's not a Baltimore Christmas unless your family is ripped on virytas."

The drink shares a great deal of similarity with the Krupnikas found in the midwestern Lithuanian communities, but virytas is pure Maryland and is traditionally made with a heavy dose of Pikesville Rye Whiskey. Though the origins are sketchy, it is most likely a "make do" recipe where immigrants simply utilized their traditional ingredients and substituted the once prevalent Maryland rye whiskey for the traditional vodka, which hadn't yet reached American shores. In a number of the more charmingly dive bars around the city, a high-octane version of virytas is created (often code-named "Evil" by the bar owners) with an Everclear or similar grain spirit base and is served up with a National Bohemian chaser.

Most virytas recipes are a closely guarded family secret, and we have had the fate of our immortal souls threatened should we divulge their exact ingredients and portions. Luckily, the following recipe appeared in a 1971 article in the *Baltimore Sun,* and with our slight modernization attempts, it is very similar to the one we cooked up with Keith Hipsley, our friend of Baltimore Lithuanian descent. The difference in ingredients was minimal—$1/4$ teaspoon minimal. Be careful when consuming. Even though this recipe isn't for the "Evil" version, the honeyed warmth can hide the punch of the rye whiskey and will hit you when you least expect it.

—⟨∾∾⟩—

# VIRYTAS

*Recipe adapted from Olga Whitehurst via the* Baltimore Sun

1 cup water
¾ cup honey
Juice of 4 lemons; rind of 1 lemon
Juice of 1 orange; rind of ½ orange
2 cinnamon sticks
1 teaspoon kummel seeds
4 cloves
1 750ml bottle of rye whiskey—traditionally Pikesville, though during Prohibition, Canadian Whisky was even used.

Heat water, honey, citrus juices, rinds and spices. Bring to a boil, then reduce heat to low. When at a very low simmer, add rye whiskey. When cool, strain into clean bottles and store in a cool place. To serve, heat on stove or microwave individual shots in the microwave for under thirty seconds.

# WHERE TO FIND VIRYTAS

LITHUANIAN HALL
851 Hollins Street
Baltimore, MD 21230
(410) 685-5787
www.lithuanianhall.com

MUMS TAVERN
1132 South Hanover Street
Baltimore, MD 21230
(410) 547-7415

# PART IV

—◦◦◦—

# PROHIBITION

## 1920–1933

## COCKTAIL TIMELINE

1918: The Eighteenth Amendment to the United States Constitution is ratified on January 6.

1919: The Volstead Act, the enabling legislation to Prohibition, is enacted.

1920: Speakeasies appear nationwide and are frequented by both sexes. The cocktail quickly spreads from the speakeasy to the American home.

1920–23: American drinking trends reverse course, and hard liquor consumption overtakes beer once again. Hypocrisy and corruption is widespread within ranks of Prohibition leaders. President Harding consumes whiskey openly on the golf course.

1932: The Twenty-first Amendment repealing Prohibition is drafted on December 6.

1933: The Cullen Bill permits the sale and consumption of beer at or below 3.2 ABV. The Eighteenth Amendment takes effect on December 5 at 4:31 p.m.

## MARYLAND TIMELINE

1917: Lithuanian Hall opens in East Baltimore.

1920: The first annual football game between future rival Catholic high schools Calvert Hall College and Loyola High School is held on November 12.

1921: Polock Johnny's is founded on the Block. Blaze Starr regularly stops by for a hot dog.

1921: Mary E.W. Risteau becomes the first woman elected to Maryland's House of Delegates.

1922: Municipal Stadium (also known as Baltimore Stadium or Venable Stadium) is built at the urging of Mayor William Frederick Broening. It will be renamed in 1954 as Memorial Stadium.

1924: Flooding destroys much of the Chesapeake and Ohio Canal.

1925: The University of Baltimore is founded.

1926: William Henry Haussner opens his eponymous Haussner's Restaurant on Eastern Avenue.

1927: The Emerson Hotel holds a dinner for Charles Lindbergh in celebration of his first solo flight across the Atlantic Ocean.

1928: Conowingo Dam is completed, crossing the lower Susquehanna River above the Head of Elk at the northern end of Chesapeake Bay. It was constructed for the Philadelphia Electric Company with a power plant, generators and turbines.

1929: Glenn L. Martin establishes an aircraft production company, east of the city at Middle River, east of Essex, in southeastern Baltimore County.

1930: Baltimore jazz singer Cab Calloway first records "Minnie the Moocher." The song become a hit one year later and popularizes the use of "hi-de-hi-de-hi-de-ho" as a catch phrase. The Baltimore Black Sox, a Negro League baseball team, plays in the first baseball game of African Americans held at old Yankee Stadium.

1931: Philanthropist Henry Walters (1848–1931) dies, leaving the famous international art collection amassed by him and his father, William T. Walters (1820–1894).

1933: A four-day storm in Ocean City cuts an inlet that becomes a permanent link between the ocean and bay, signaling the dawn of the town's prominence as a sport fishing center.

1934: The Walters Art Gallery opens to the public.

# CHAPTER 11

# PROHIBITION IN MARYLAND

In the yearlong run-up to the start of Prohibition, the Volstead Act had a provision that allowed private citizens to keep whatever alcohol they previously had on hand, so there was a mad dash to buy up all of the hard spirits they could find. In Baltimore, wholesalers scrambled to load whatever they could into ships in Sparrows Point waiting to ship out to prearranged offshore warehouses in Nassau.

After the ratification of the Eighteenth Amendment and its enabling legislation, the National Prohibition (aka Volstead) Act, each state was granted the right to enact its own concurrent legislation, with the provision that it was at least as stringent as the federal law. Ironically, Maryland, the sixth state to ratify national Prohibition, was quick to desert the cause and refused to pass any statewide enforcement measures. It would be the only state in the Union to follow this course and soon became the "wettest" state in the land. The backlash to the unpopular law was swift in coming, and by the time of enforcement, 50 percent of the Maryland senators and 90 percent of the state delegates, as well as then governor Emerson C. Harrington, had been voted out of office.

Harrington's successor, Governor Albert C. Ritchie, was a staunch opponent of Prohibition and an outward supporter of the "wet" cause. Making the matter a states' rights issue, he wanted Marylanders to have the freedom to decide for themselves about the morality of alcohol consumption. The *Baltimore Sun* echoed this sentiment and argued that the Eighteenth Amendment endangered the Tenth Amendment, which protected the

*Left*: Maryland governor Albert C. Ritchie. Harris & Ewing Collection. *Library of Congress.*

*Below*: H.L. Mencken. *Library of Congress.*

individual rights of the states. Leading the opposition, Vincent Palmisano, John Phillip Hill and Senator Millard Tydings submitted one repeal bill after another to keep up the pressure on their "dry" adversaries.

When issues of Maryland's patriotism were brought into question, one *Sun* writer shot back by coining the moniker the "Maryland Free State." The paper would continue to condemn Prohibition throughout its lifespan, especially under the watch of H.L. Mencken.

Of the leading agitators, Harvard-educated three-time Republican congressman John Phillip Hill had the most deliberate run-ins with the law. In 1924, Hill purposely got himself arrested in order to challenge the language in the law that allowed farmers to ferment for home use any fruit they produced to a maximum ABV of 2.75 percent, taking issue that this same right was not extended to city dwellers who lacked land and could not purchase any beverage over 1 percent alcohol. A statement in the April 22, 1923 edition of the *Baltimore Sun* described Hill's plan in detail:

> *Congressman John Phillip Hill today served formal and solemn notice on the Probation Commissioner and the Collector of Internal Revenue for Maryland that on or about noon, September 7, he will begin producing non-intoxicating* [sic] *fruit juices for use in his home. His intention is to get from the prohibition department a definition of "non-intoxicating" as used in the Volstead Act.*
>
> *When the new regulations concerning the manufacture for home use of cider and similar fruit juices were issued; he said, "I expect to find the definition in them. But after reading them carefully I find that 'non-intoxicating' is defined simply as 'non-intoxicating.'*
>
> *So, I'm going up in the country and get some grapes and go down on Baltimore Street and get a press, and I'm going to start making grape juice. I have written the Prohibition Commissioner to ask him just when I should stop fermentation. In his answer I expect to learn after two years of inquiry just when a beverage ceases to be non-intoxicating and becomes intoxicating."*

A picture would emerge of Hill days later, showing him in possession of baskets of grapes obtained from right around the state capitol.

Hill would try his hand at cider making for his next stunt. In the courtyard attached to his Baltimore City residence at 3 West Franklin Street, he planted five apple trees (though some accounts state that he merely tied apples to the branches of existing trees) to create an "orchard" in an attempt to make hard cider up to the 2.75 percent limit. This time,

Congressman John Phillip Hill. National Photo Company Collection. *Library of Congress.*

Hill was arrested, but the charge would ultimately be thrown out by Judge Morris A. Soper. The trial made national news and was a publicity nightmare for "drys," but Prohibition would still drag on for another nine years. Baltimore kept on drinking. Upon Hill's death in 1941, the *Baltimore Evening Sun* stated, "At the Farms he had five apple trees and two beautiful grapevines…and from the home cultivation of these plants he managed to fill his cellar with their liquid products"—not too shabby for an amateur viticulturist!

Understandably, authentic Prohibition-era recipes are hard to find, but luckily, two of Hill's personal recipes were preserved in Frederick Philip Stieff's 1932 recipe collection, *Eat, Drink and Be Merry in Maryland.* The combination rum/brandy eggnog and punch are pretty standard affairs as far as Maryland drink recipes go, but what better way to toast the next Repeal Day than with a glass of cheer once served up by Maryland's greatest "wet"?

---

## FRANKLIN FARMS RUM PUNCH

*Recipe by John Phillip Hill, Franklin Farms, Baltimore, Maryland*

12 lemons
1¾ pounds lump sugar
1 quart strong green unpowered tea
1 quart old Jamaica rum

Put sugar in large bowl and squeeze the juice of the lemons over the sugar; throw the rinds in another large bowl to use later—

mixing the tea by scalding the teapot and putting in one-eighth pound of tea, fill the pot with boiling water and let this draw for twenty (20) minutes by the clock; pour one quart of hot tea over the lemon's rinds and let stand for ten (10) minutes; then pour the hot tea from the rinds into the lemon juice and sugar. When the sugar is dissolved, pour in the quart of Jamaica rum and put in a demi-john and cork tightly. This should stand twenty-four (24) hours. Fill bowl with crushed ice and pour the punch over it.

# SPEAKEASIES

As the center of state (and, arguably, national) resistance, Baltimore City was a hotspot for illegal drinking establishments. Frequently raided by federal agents, as Baltimore cops easily turned a blind eye, the speakeasies rebounded quickly and opened soon after the disturbance as if nothing happened. One of the most famous examples was located in what is now the Owl Bar within the Belvedere. Aside from some recent (and necessary) renovations, the décor has changed little since the time of the "Noble Experiment."

# MOONSHINING IN THE WEST, RUMRUNNING ON THE CHESAPEAKE

During the years of Prohibition, Western Maryland farmers and enterprising "mountain folk" were quick to supplement their income by reverting to the time-honored practice of cranking out homemade whiskey from family-run distillery operations, as small stills were easier to hide than large beer operations. At the same time, smugglers in fast-moving boats skulked along several hundred miles of Maryland coastline to deliver their illicit cargo.

The wilderness of the Eastern Shore, prior to the construction of the Bay Bridge, was a complex maze of creeks and rivers. It provided ample cover for numerous bootlegging endeavors, and backcountry moonshine was easily smuggled out and into the entire region. Despite a few federal raids, most operations weathered until repeal, and some lasted well into the 1950s, particularly if local law enforcement was adequately paid off or directly involved.

# THE GREAT WHISKEY HEIST

Early in January 1926, fifty men pulled off one of the greatest whiskey heists in American history. In an act that was one part *Ocean's Eleven*, one part *Boardwalk Empire*, they were able to carry away over seventy barrels and thirty-two cases of bottles containing aged rye whiskey from the government-held site of the former Arthur McGinnis Distillery. Now twenty-one years after its closing, the McGinnis plant was then being used as a storage site, and the rye whiskey was being doled out little by little for "medicinal purposes."

The caper began with three men disguised as ice skaters who walked up to the federal government–employed guard, held him at gunpoint and then tied him up. Also taken hostage at the time was an eighty-year-old man who was looking for his lost cat and was simply at the wrong place at the wrong time. When the rest of the crew arrived, they made short work of the remaining seven watchmen and, for the next fifteen hours, loaded five trucks up the with rye whiskey, then valued at over $90,000 dollars.

When federal agents finally caught on, the trucks and their escort of mobsters in cars were already on their way to Mexico. Eventually, seven men believed to be associated with the heist were arrested on separate bootlegging charges, though accounts are unclear if they were ever charged with this particular crime.

Following the theft, the government relocated the remnants of the whiskey to another location and had the Arthur McGinnis facility demolished.

———

## MILLARD TYDINGS'S KENTUCKY BREAKFAST

*As a meal familiar to bartenders around the world, Maryland Senator Millard Tydings offered his recipe for a Kentucky breakfast, found in Stieff's* Eat, Drink and Be Merry in Maryland:

> *This potation, to be thoroughly enjoyed, should be prepared in the following manner:*
>
> *Supply each guest with a glass containing about one-half inch of water and one-quarter teaspoonful of sugar, and a spoon.*
>
> *All should sit comfortably and stir the sugar until it is thoroughly dissolved. The host should tell the following story in a low voice while the sugar is being stirred:*
>
> *"Have you gentlemen ever participated at a Kentucky breakfast?"*
>
> *The answer is likely to be in the negative.*

Senator Millard Tydings. Harris & Ewing Collection. *Library of Congress.*

Then some guest will probably ask:

*"What is a Kentucky breakfast?"*

At this point the sugar is completely dissolved. The host passes around a bottle of Bourbon and each person pours into his glass, containing the dissolved sugar, such amount as suits his inclination. This is stirred for a while, during which time the most replies:

*"A Kentucky breakfast is a big beefsteak, a quart of Bourbon, and a houn' dawg."*

One of the guests will then ask: *"What is the dog for?"*

The host then replies: *"He eats the beefsteak."*

Ice water is then passed around in a silver pitcher to dilute drink to meet the requirements of the discriminating taste of each. A part of the Kentucky breakfast is then consumed.

(In order to extract the nth power of enjoyment from this receipt, when stirring the sugar and water, each should sit on the very edge of his chair or sofa, rest his arms on his knees with a slightly forward posture. Unless this is done the drink will taste just a little less good.)

# PART V

# THE POST-REPEAL ERA

## 1934–1969

The repeal of the Eighteenth Amendment was welcomed with fanfare in the state of Maryland. In Baltimore, H.L. Mencken, in the run-up to full repeal, enjoyed the "official" legal beer at the Rennert Hotel's bar. But the long years of Prohibition took their toll on the Maryland rye industry: although some distilleries rose from the ashes, tastes had changed to milder flavors as a result, and the onset of World War II brought soldiers back from the Pacific with a taste for the exotic.

In the rest of the country, the tiki craze arrived, ushered in by Don Beach and Trader Vic. The Bloody Mary, Mai Tai, vodka martini and vesper all appear during this era.

## COCKTAIL TIMELINE

1934: Fernand Petiot, one of the many alleged creators of the Bloody Mary, becomes head bartender at the King Cole Bar in the St. Regis New York. Don Beach (born Ernest Raymond Beaumont Gantt) opens a bar called Don the Beachcomber in Hollywood, California

1936: Victor Bergeron changes the name of his bar Hinky Dinks to Trader Vic's.

1942: With America active in World War II, sugar rationing begins on the homefront, and U.S. distillery production is diverted to the war effort. Rum and Coca-Cola are affordable and in good supply.

1944: Victor Bergeron creates the Mai Tai.

1951: *Bottoms Up* by Ted Saucier includes a recipe of vodka and dry vermouth mixed 4:1 called the Vodkatini, credited to Jerome Zerbe, the first society photographer, notorious for stalking celebrities at the Rainbow Room and El Morocco nightclubs in Manhattan.

1953: The margarita appears in print for the first time in *Esquire Magazine*. The vesper appears in Ian Fleming's *Casino Royale* and is forever linked to the world of James Bond.

## MARYLAND TIMELINE

1933: Wendell Wilson opens the Vilma Tavern on Pennsylvania Avenue.

1936: F. Scott Fitzgerald checks into room 409 at the Stafford Hotel and runs up a heady $22.35 bill at the hotel's bar and restaurant. "George," a bartender at the Emerson, creates the Preakness cocktail.

1945: Former *Baltimore Sun* journalist Philip Wagner opens Boordy Vineyards.

1951: The Diamondback cocktail is mentioned in Ted Saucier's book, *Bottoms Up*.

1952: The Chesapeake Bay Bridge opens.

1958: The Hawaiian Room opens at the Hotel Emerson.

## CHAPTER 12

# COCKTAILS ON THE AVENUE

## PENNSYLVANIA AVENUE BLACK NIGHTCLUBS

### THE VILMA TAVERN

*Any connoisseur of good drinks will readily agree that Wendell has the best mixed drinks in Baltimore.*
*—Peyton Gray for the* Afro-American

In 1933, Wendell Alexander Wilson, the "Dean of Baker Street," opened the high-end Vilma Tavern on the corner of Baltimore's Pennsylvania Avenue and Baker Street. It was one of the first bars in the city to be owned and operated by an African American.

Born in 1898, Wendell Wilson was the son of Robert Wilson, an aide to then Baltimore mayor Ferdinand Claiborne Latrobe, and his wife, Mary. After high school, Wilson attended Morgan College and then went to New York University in pursuit of a medical degree. Unfortunately, his plans were interrupted when he was drafted into the United States Army and was sent overseas, where he saw action in the final phase of the Battle of the Argonne.

Upon his return home to Baltimore, Wilson resumed work at the newsstand he had set up during his college years on North and Pennsylvania Avenues, where he sold newspapers, popular magazines and candy, as well as offering hat cleaning and shoe shining services. In 1933, he sold the eighteen-year-old business in order to make way for his dream of opening the Vilma.

From the outset, the forward-thinking Wilson sought to make the Vilma Tavern "a clean, well-managed place where cultured folk could gather and spend a pleasant evening sipping expertly mixed drinks amid a friendly atmosphere." Using his business training, he searched out and visited many of the "hotcha spots" around town and studied their operations and business practices before opening his own establishment. Peyton Gray, in a 1938 article for the *Afro-American*, had this to say about Wilson's vision: "His theory for conducting a successful business is to sell his patrons what they want, the way they want it in the best manner possible. Patrons should be treated as friends rather than stepping stones to prosperity, he thinks."

After opening, the Vilma Tavern became a fixture on the southwest corner of Pennsylvania Avenue and Baker Street, with a hard-to-miss neon sign luring patrons into either the "spick and span" barroom or the "cozy" booths that lined the rear wall of the building, where guests could enjoy their expertly made drinks away from raucous crowds in the quiet of the Vilma's sophisticated atmosphere.

The bar team, known locally as "the white coat boys," changed little over the course of time and was headed up by the smiling and gracious bar manager Charlie Carr, mixologist Edward "Mex" Plater and Riley (it is uncertain whether this is was his first name or surname), the bartender. All were frequently regarded as some of the best "concoctionists" in the area, who always paid careful attention to preparing drinks in the proper way and serving them at the proper temperature. Specific drinks that received frequent accolades in the local nightlife columns were whiskey sours, the "Joe Louis Punch" and even the Frozen Rye.

The in-house entertainment was provided nightly by Kitty West on the piano, band members Georgia Paul and Howard Turner and "newcomer" Dot Turner on vocals.

Despite the expertise and quality of his staff, Wilson was always the centerpiece of the Vilma's appeal. To many regulars, he was "the prince of good fellows" with a magnetic personality and a smile that was the "great consoler" to those who spilled out their troubles to him.

—⊸◌◌◌⊷—

# THE VILMA SPECIAL

*Re-created from a description in the May 25, 1935 edition of the* Baltimore Afro-American *newspaper. It was credited to a bartender named "Crisp."*

1½ ounces gin (the original was probably Buchu or Dixie Bell, both extinct brands)
orange juice
juice of half a lemon
seltzer water

Build over ice in a chilled Collins or highball glass.

# CHAPTER 13

# 1936:

# THE PREAKNESS COCKTAIL

## THE ORIGINAL DRINK OF PIMLICO

Prior to the Black-Eyed Susan's introduction as the official drink of the second jewel in Thoroughbred racing's Triple Crown, Maryland racing fans sang the praises of another cocktail: the Preakness. Long before the faux-centaur Kegasus, "Lord of InfieldFest," trotted among his legion of binge-drinking partygoers, the Preakness festivities were more of a society affair, and the first Preakness Ball in 1936 proved legendary.

In late April 1936, five judges gathered in the John Eager Howard Room of the Belvedere Hotel to choose the signature cocktail of the upcoming Preakness Ball. Led by none other than John Phillip Hill, the panel had to choose from a field of eight cocktails, all dreamed up by some of Baltimore's "ablest mixers," as the room's organ played softly in the background. One of the team, Mrs. Bruce Collen, divulged that prior to this occasion, she had never even tasted a cocktail before, an omission that earned her a kiss on the hand by former congressman John Philip Hill.

At 4:00 p.m. sharp, Hill called the panel to order as Clerk of the Courts David F. Wood read out the rules of the competition. Of the total score, 25 percent would be for "conformity," which included the "beauty" and "bouquet" of the drink, while the remaining 75 percent would go to "performance"—the taste and "effect." Hill quickly stated that he was perfectly fine with all of the criteria but that he was especially "okay with the last one."

Very few details were given about each cocktail, and nothing even approaching actual recipes was recorded. Cocktail #1 was brought out to the tune of "How Dry I Am," and Hill, once he had finished tasting, pronounced that it was "superb." He would have the same to say of Cocktail #2, a "pale yellow" concoction served up while the tune "Horses, Crazy Over Horses" played. The third drink—merely described as cloudy, red and sipped slowly by the judges—is the only one that bears any stated resemblance to the Preakness cocktail known today. After the third entry had finished, the pace of the judging picked up, and Cocktails #4–8 were consumed in far quicker succession. Once the winner had been chosen (we are never told exactly which entry number won), John Phillip Hill raised his glass, saluted the portrait of John Eager Howard and gave a final pronouncement of "superb." In a 2009 article in *Malt Advocate*, spirits writer David Wondrich reveals that the drink was created by George (his last name is lost to history), the head bartender at the Emerson Hotel.

The newly dubbed Preakness cocktail would make its debut on May 16, 1936, at the Preakness Ball, where a team of fifty veteran decorators transformed the interior of the Fifth Regiment Armory into a replica of the Pimlico racetrack. The *Baltimore Sun* articles that week gave accounts that the affair may one day "compete in beauty and brilliancy" with such events as the Kentucky Derby and Mardi Gras and that "every effort would be made" to repeat the occasion for subsequent Preaknesses. Among the "dazzling throng" of over five thousand attendees was the cream of Baltimore's political and social elite, who arrived by expensive chauffeured automobiles. Once inside, the guests were greeted by Billy Barton and Dr. Freeland, two of Maryland's retired champion horses, chomping on oats in the Armory lobby. In the ballroom, the ceiling had been painted a sky blue, and the walls were "foliage green" with silver floor-to-ceiling panels placed at twenty-one-foot intervals, adorned with the silhouettes of the forty-five previous victors. The well-to-do took their places in one of eighty-six green-and-white boxes made up to represent the horse stalls, while the remainder of the attendees took their place at one of the hundreds of tables that ringed the dance floor "track."

At 11:30 p.m., the Preakness Court arrived, headed up by Mrs. W.W. Lanham, who had been crowned the queen of Preakness Week, resplendent in a white satin gown with a lace-trimmed bouffant skirt. On her shoulder, she wore an epaulette of orange, the official race color. The queen's entourage included two princesses and ten duchesses representing various counties around the state. Lawrence Tibbet of the Metropolitan Opera presided over the coronation and crowned Mrs. Lanham as she sat on a chair used by Queen Marie of Romania during her visit to the Belvedere Hotel.

All told, the Preakness Ball required two large orchestras; eight thousand glasses "of all descriptions" to accommodate the various highballs, cocktails and champagne consumed; thirty bartenders manning six separate bars; and 150 waitstaff led by sixteen captains.

Throughout the evening, the Preakness cocktail was said to have "flowed like water," but the drink doesn't even warrant a mention in the news coverage of the following year's ball, relegated to a Hornick's Seafood Restaurant spot advertising the drink for twenty-five cents. By 1966, race fans would "search in vain" for any bar that still served the drink. David Wondrich attributes this to the fact that "drinks that win cocktail contests almost never achieve lasting, and rarely even fleeting, popularity."

⟋⟋⟋⟋

## THE PREAKNESS COCKTAIL

*The following recipe is a simplified version but still very similar to traditional recipe recorded in most cocktail books. By all accounts, it's simply a Manhattan variant—George the bartender apparently played it safe—with the simple addition of a dash of the honey-herbal liqueur Bénédictine. Recipe adapted from David Wondrich.*

2 ounces straight rye whiskey

1 ounce Martini & Rossi red vermouth

2 dashes Angostura bitters (though some early versions substitute Peychauds)

½ teaspoon Bénédictine

Stir with cracked ice. Strain into a chilled cocktail glass, and twist a swatch of thin-cut lemon peel over the top.

# CHAPTER 14

# 1951:
# THE DIAMONDBACK LOUNGE

The recipe for the Diamondback first appears in Ted Saucier's *Bottoms Up*, a Truman-era classic from 1951. Saucier describes the drink as two parts Old Schenley rye whiskey, with one part each of applejack and yellow Chartreuse. Saucier, the publicist for the Waldorf-Astoria hotel in New York, collected the best of the era's cocktails from a variety of sources ranging from celebrities to bar staff.

Located one level down from the lobby in what is now the space shared by LB Bakery and the French Kitchen in the Lord Baltimore Hotel, the Diamondback Lounge closed in the late 1970s but was described as a piano bar with red shag carpet emblazoned with the signature turtle logo. Oddly enough, the 1956 cocktail menu fails to list the Diamondback as an option.

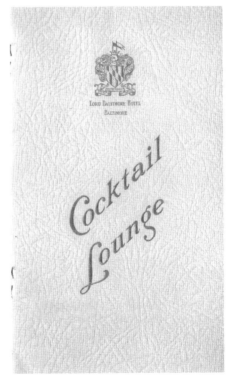

Lord Baltimore cocktail menu. *Authors' collection.*

| COCKTAILS | |
|---|---|
| Lord Baltimore | .50 |
| Alexander | .50 |
| Jack Rose | .50 |
| Clover Club | .40 |
| Ward Eight | .50 |
| Stinger | .50 |
| Side Car | .50 |
| Frog Hop | .50 |
| Coffee | .60 |
| Bacardi | .40 |
| Daiquiri | .40 |
| Three Dagger | .40 |
| Old Fashioned | .40 |
| Dubonnet | .35 |
| Blue Moon | .40 |
| Sazarac | .40 |
| Manhattan | .30 |
| Martini | .25 |
| Bronx | .25 |
| Queens | .25 |
| Orange Blossom | .25 |
| Champagne (for 2) | 1.00 |
| La President | .50 |

**TALL DRINKS**

| | |
|---|---|
| Gin Daisy | .45 |
| Mint Julep | .50 |
| Frozen Bacardi | .50 |
| Frozen Ron Rico | .50 |
| Tom Collins | .40 |
| Gin Rickey | .35 |
| Sloe Gin Rickey | .35 |

**PUNCHES**

| | |
|---|---|
| West India Punch | .50 |
| Brandy Egg Nog | .75 |
| Planters Punch | .50 |
| Milk Punch | .45 |
| Milk Punch with Egg | .50 |
| Brandy Milk Punch | .75 |
| Claret Punch | .40 |

**FIZZES**

| | |
|---|---|
| Gin Fizz | .40 |
| Royal Fizz | .50 |
| Silver Fizz | .50 |
| Golden Fizz | .50 |
| New Orleans Fizz | .75 |

**WHISKEYS**

| | |
|---|---|
| Bonded Rye | .35  .40 and  .60 |
| Straight or Blend Rye | .30 |
| Scotch | .40  .45 and  .50 |

Straight or High Ball

**LIQUEURS** — Pony

| | |
|---|---|
| Apricot Brandy | .35 |
| Anisette | .35 |
| Benedictine | .40 |
| Chartreuse Yellow | .40 |
| Chartreuse Green | .50 |
| Creme de Cacao | .35 |
| Cointreau | .40 |
| Grand Marnier | .50 |
| Creme Yvette | .35 |
| Creme de Menthe White | .35 |
| Creme de Menthe Green | .35 |

WE SERVE ONLY IMPORTED CORDIALS

**BRANDIES** — Pony

| | |
|---|---|
| Courvoisier V. S. | .35 |
| Hennessy ★★★ | .35 |
| Morton | .35 |

**BEERS, ALES and STOUTS**

| | |
|---|---|
| Local | .15 |
| Budweiser | .25 |
| Pabst | .25 |
| Schlitz | .25 |
| Dogs Head Bass | .50 |
| Guiness Stout | .50 |
| Jolly Scot | .15 |
| Ballantines | .25 |

Lord Baltimore Hotel cocktail menu, circa 1950. *Authors' collection.*

---

# THE DIAMONDBACK

*Recipe from* Bottoms Up, *by Ted Saucier*

two parts Old Schenley rye whiskey
one part applejack
one part yellow Chartreuse

Shake well. Serve over ice in old-fashioned glass. Decorate with
sprig of fresh mint.

## WHERE TO GET THE DIAMONDBACK

BOOKMAKERS COCKTAIL CLUB
31 East Cross Street
Baltimore, MD 21230

LB TAVERN AT THE LORD BALTIMORE HOTEL
20 West Baltimore Street
Baltimore, MD 21201

## CHAPTER 15

# 1958–1971:
# THE HAWAIIAN ROOM

W‍ho would have guessed that from 1958 to 1971, Baltimore had its very own Trader Vic–style tiki bar? Located in what was the former barbershop of the Emerson Hotel on the corner of Baltimore and North Calvert Streets, the Hawaiian room was described as "Baltimore's most California effort in the supper club business." Sparing no expense, the owners went over budget by almost $40,000 to bedeck the interior in blowfish-shaped lamps and authentic lava rock and coral shipped in from "the islands."

As for cuisine, the Hawaiian room was the height of faux-Polynesian and served the finest Asian-inspired dishes designed specifically for the 1960s American palate. The drink menu was graced with the likes of many a tiki classic and includes such greats as the Singapore Sling, Scorpion Bowl, Navy Grog, Zombie and even its version of the still-secret Mai Tai (Trader Vic wouldn't publish his recipe until after the closure of the Hawaiian Room) all served up in ceramic pineapples, tiki mugs and deaths heads. As they dined and sipped the night away, guests were entertained by many talented performers, including fire dancers and hula girls.

The Emerson and the Hawaiian room bore witness to two relatively famous civil rights cases. On February 8, 1963, William D. Zantzinger, the rich young son of a wealthy tobacco farmer, struck Hattie Carroll, an African American fifty-one-year-old cocktail waitress over the head with his cane. The mother of eleven children died at Mercy Hospital just a few hours later. Zantzinger had arrived to the scene already drunk and assaulted another employee before Carroll. Court records state that he

14567. New Emerson Hotel,
Baltimore and
Calvert Streets,
Baltimore, Md.

Emerson Hotel. *Authors' collection.*

*Above*: Hawaiian Room staff, including Meki (front row, center) and JoAnn "Wainani" To'alepais (front row, right). *Courtesy of the To'alepais family.*

HEAD HUNTER SPECIAL . 1.65
Light Rum, Dark Rum, Pineapple and Grapefruit J u i c e, Topped with Brandy

*Left*: A tiki-inspired drink, served up in one of the Hawaiian Room's many special glasses. *Courtesy of the To'alepais family.*

struck her because she paused for a second or two longer than he wanted while making his drink. To make the tragic story worse, Zantzinger was only charged with manslaughter and received a mere six-month jail sentence. The story would be forever immortalized in the Bob Dylan song "The Lonesome Death of Hattie Carroll," released the following year:

*William Zanzinger killed poor Hattie Carroll*
*With a cane that he twirled around his diamond ring finger*
*At a Baltimore hotel society gath'rin'*
*And the cops were called in and his weapon took from him*

**134**

*As they rode him in custody down to the station*
*And booked William Zanzinger for first-degree murder*
*But you who philosophize disgrace and criticize all fears*
*Take the rag away from your face*
*Now ain't the time for your tears.*

On a lighter note, the Hawaiian room itself played host to the love story between Meki To'alepais, a performer from a well-known traveling Polynesian show, and JoAnn Kovacs, a local hula dancer from Locust Point. In December 1963, Meki was performing with the dance troupe, and JoAnn caught his eye as she swayed to the music. Long story short, the couple soon planned to marry but found themselves blocked by Maryland's 1935 miscegenation law. Meki, of Samoan ancestry, couldn't marry JoAnn in state because the law didn't allow white women to marry so-called brown men. Not willing to wait for the law to change, they exchanged vows on February 19, 1966, in Washington, D.C., instead. As a consolation, the To'alepaises did hold an appropriately Polynesian-themed reception in Hampden. Today, their son, Meki, carries on the family tradition and runs a local island-themed dance group.

Matchbook from the Emerson Hotel. *Authors' collection.*

## WHERE TO FIND THE FORMER SITE OF THE HAWAIIAN ROOM

4 North Charles Street
Baltimore, MD 21201

# CHAPTER 16

# THE SOUTHSIDE

*The Southside, a tangy cocktail made with mint, citrus juices and secrets,
is an old-line favorite.*
—*Rob Kasper*

The Southside cocktail is the king of the Maryland Hunt Club tailgate, and its season stretches from the April Hunt Cup all the way through white-shoe weather and into Labor Day weekend. Avid fan George Barnhill summed up the cocktail's allure: "It's associated with horse racing and warm weather…A Southside means the rebirth of a new season." Indeed, most Steeplechase aficionados won't consider their picnic hamper complete without a stop off at Graul's Market for a bottle of Mr. Harold's or Lindsay's Southside mix.

So how does an out-of-state drink, reputedly the work of Chicago gangsters, migrate to the Hamptons and then become the darling of preppies everywhere and a fixture of the set? The true story is up for debate, but no one will argue the undeniable appeal of this "sunshine sweet elixir" during the sometimes sweltering Maryland summers.

In 2004, NPR's *Day by Day* profiled the Southside, noting its status as the "definitive drink of the country club set." Apparently, the drink got its name from Joe Saltis and Frankie McErlane, two Prohibition-era gangsters who mixed up a solution of citrus and mint to mask the off-flavors of their illicit booze. The Southside eventually proved so popular that it soon popped up in New York City at Jack & Charley's speakeasy—named for the two

Austrian owners—and even the famous 21 Club. It's a great tale, but like most cocktail origin stories, it has no evidence to back it up and plenty to the contrary. The most plausible history, according to longtime *Washington Post* writer Eric Felten, credits the Southside Sportsmen's Club that opened in the 1870s on Long Island. Elizabeth Foster adds more evidence in a October 1941 article in *Town & Country* in which she remarks on the club's mint-centric menu and mentions the Southside by name as "a Tom Collins with mint [that] is cooling in warm weather." The first printed recipe appears in the 1930 edition of Harry Craddock's *The Savoy Cocktail Book* and is described simply as "mint shaken with gin, lemon juice, ice and sugar."

In Maryland, the Greenspring Valley Hunt Club claims that it has been serving the Southside since 1929, but we can only definitively trace the Southside to the early 1960s in the Baltimore area. Here, the Southside swaps out the original gin base for rum, and this version appears to be completely "peculiar to Baltimore." For the rum, the authentic choice has always been the sailor's favorite, Mount Gay, usually one of the dark varieties, though Meyers Dark Rum has also seen use.

Throughout the Baltimore area, Southside fans draw squarely up into two contentious camps: that of George Lee or Andy Ervin. Lee, a one-time butler and head bartender at Greenspring Valley from 1969 to 1985, states that his version was inspired by a recipe printed in an old Long Island Club book. Lee had mixed up a batch of Southsides while working at the Ten Mile House on Reisterstown Road, prior to its closing in 1967, but remarked that the cocktail was slow to catch on with the clientele. The drink only took off once he started serving it at Greenspring Valley. Lee retired in 1985 but still works the occasional private event, devoting most of his time to mixing up home batches of his proprietary Southside mix, which he supplies to local bartenders by the thirty-two-ounce bottle. In the other corner of the debate is the ninety-something Andy Ervin, head bartender (still) at the Elkridge Club on North Charles Street, who has been serving up his take on the Southside since 1961, the recipe a result of his experiments during the development of the club's mixed-drink program.

The differences between the Greenspring Valley and the Elkridge Southsides lie mostly with method rather than ingredients. George Lee deliberately uses only the leaves of the mint in his mix and sticks with the original lemon, resulting in a golden color with a citrusy, sweet taste. Andy Ervin pulverizes the mint, stems and all, and uses a combination of lemon and lime, resulting in an almost glowing green color.

Once a jealously guarded secret, the Southside recipe has thankfully escaped into the public sphere. Below are two recipes that showcase the many subtle variations of this classic. Also be sure to check out the "Maryland Cider and Spirits" section of the book for details on how to obtain the many Southside bottled mixes available in Maryland.

## ANDY ERVIN'S SOUTHSIDE

*Recipe adapted from Rob Kasper, the* Baltimore Sun

1 "heavin' handful" of mint cuttings (about 2 cups)
3 ounces fresh-squeezed lemon juice
4 ounces fresh-squeezed lime juice
8 tablespoons granulated sugar
8 ice cubes
rum (traditionally Mount Gay or Meyers Dark)

Place every ingredient, except the rum, in a blender or food processor and run on high until mint is chopped, about thirty to sixty seconds. Strain, pouring mixture into a pitcher. For each drink, fill a 12-ounce glass with ice. Add 4 ounces of mint mixture and 3 ounces of rum. Stir well. Top with a shot of dark rum. Makes enough for four 12-ounce cocktails.

## AARON JOSEPH'S BALTIMORE SOUTHSIDE

*For a twenty-first-century take on the classic, Aaron Joseph, head bartender at Wit & Wisdom in Harbor East, provided us with his updated rendition of the Southside. This version leans more toward the original* Savoy Cocktail Book *recipe and would be easy for any would-be-mixologist to make at home.*

1½ ounces of Papa's Pilar Blonde Rum
¾ ounce lemon
½ ounce cane syrup
10 to 12 mint leaves

Place all ingredients in cocktail shaker including the mint. Add ice. Shake vigorously. Double strain into cocktail coupe. Garnish with mint.

## WHERE TO GET A SOUTHSIDE

Elkridge Club
6100 North Charles Street
Baltimore, MD 21212
(410) 377-9200

Greenspring Valley Hunt Club
30 Greenspring Valley Road
Owings Mills, MD 21117
(410) 363-0433

Wit & Wisdom
A Modern American Tavern by Michael Mina
200 International Avenue
Baltimore, MD 21202
(410) 576-5800

# PART VI

⟫⟫⟫⟫⟫

# THE DARK AGE OF THE COCKTAIL

## 1970–1985

In the 1960s and into the '70s, American youth culture sought to buck the establishment and distance themselves from the societal norms and values of the 1950s. In their rejection of all things that harkened back to their parents' generation, the classic cocktail was seen as a "square" symbol of the archaic past. The martini gave way to overly simplified, commercial sour mix and sugar–dominated drinks designed to mask any trace of alcohol. In the spirits world, vodka unseated whiskey for the first time in American history and reigned supreme. The war on flavor raged into the early 1980s.

1960: Lager beer rises in popularity; it would reach its peak in 1990.
1966: Mississippi repeals statewide prohibition. It is the last state to do so.
1970: The Harvey Wallbanger appears.
1974: Bailey's Irish Cream rises in popularity partly due to the introduction of the Mudslide drink.
1976: Vodka becomes the most popular spirit in America.
1977: The microbrewery movement begins in Sonoma, California.
1978: Home brewing is legalized for the first time since 1920.
1984: DeKuyper releases Peachtree Schnapps, a vital component in a Fuzzy Navel.
1985: Wine coolers become all the rage in the United States. The Woo Woo and Sex on the Beach appear.

# MARYLAND TIMELINE

1963: Center Stage opens on East North Avenue in Baltimore.

1966: The Baltimore Orioles win the World Series against defending champs, the Los Angeles Dodgers.

1968: The Baltimore Riots occur April 6–14.

1970: The Ott House Pub opens in Emmitsburg, Maryland.

1971: William Donald Schaeffer becomes the mayor of Baltimore.

1973: The Black-Eyed Susan is developed for the Preakness by the Heulbein Company.

1976: The Maryland Science Center opens.

1979: The Baltimore Convention Center opens.

1980: Harborplace opens.

1981: The National Aquarium opens.

1982: The Joseph Meyerhoff Symphony Hall opens.

# CHAPTER 17

# NO RESPECT

## THE SAD CASE OF THE BLACK-EYED SUSAN

*Take vodka, rum, whiskey, bourbon, peach schnapps, orange juice, pineapple juice,*
*sour mix, orange-flavored liqueur, elderflower-flavored liqueur, shake, pour into*
*a souvenir glass and garnish with an orange slice, cherry and mint sprig. Then*
*dump it on the infield grass and get a real drink.*
—*Richard Gorelick,* Baltimore Sun, *May 12, 2014*

The history of the Black-Eyed Susan is relatively brief. In 1973, to mark the centennial of the Preakness, Pimlico caterers Harry M. Stevens Co. contracted the Heulbein Company—a giant in the ready-to-drink home cocktail market—to help them create a quick and ready pre-mix to serve the expected crowds, and some expected thousands. What they came up with is described on the Retro Baltimore website as "a base of rum and vodka, splashed with orange and pineapple juices."

When introduced, the print advertisements, filled with sophisticates in Edwardian attire, weaved a tall tale, claiming that the cocktail hearkened back to the early days of the Maryland Jockey club. The reality proved to be "a mixture more Madison Avenue than a bartender." The wording from the ad was as follows:

> *Said to be the invention of a daring horse-owning notable in the early days*
> *of the Maryland Jockey club, the Black Eyed Susan, the official drink of*
> *the famed Preakness Stakes, is a tradition at Pimlico.*

*It's a bold and racy kind of drink with a clean start and an unflagging finish.*
*As exhilarating as a golden day at the track.*

Pimlico soon parted ways with Heublein, which, upon departure, refused to divulge the actual recipe for the drink's base mixture (legend states that it was later repackaged as the infamous Brass Monkey). Though the Susan itself was never popular, people did buy it every year in order to score one of the limited-edition glasses it came in. So Pimlico came up with its own formula. How close it was to the 1973 original? We will never know, but drinks writer Ted Haigh was able to dig up an early version of Pimlico's recipe:

—◈◈◈—

## BLACK-EYED SUSAN (ORIGINAL)

*Recipe adapted from Ted Haigh*

1 ounce vodka
1 ounce Mount Gay Eclipse rum
¾ ounce Cointreau
1½ ounces fresh-squeezed orange juice
1½ ounces pineapple juice

Build in a Collins glass filled with crushed ice. Add a Maraschino cherry, an orange wheel, a pineapple cube and a lime wedge for garnishes. Note: It's imperative to squeeze the juice from the lime wedge into the drink.

Like any good marketing venture, the Black-Eyed Susan recipe served trackside morphed over time to suit the evolving tastes of the increasingly younger and less sophisticated crowd drawn to the Preakness, as well as the changing corporate liquor sponsorships. Bourbon and rum came and went over the years, and at times it appeared that the only constant in the cocktail was the inclusion of vodka and pineapple juice. Most bizarrely, the recipes of the early 2000s contained white crème de menthe and brandy.

In 1987, *Baltimore Sun* writer Rob "The Happy Eater" Kasper challenged the reign of the Black-Eyed Susan and presided over the "Stick It to the

Susan" contest to choose a better cocktail to represent the Preakness. Kasper himself was no fan of the Susan, which he described as "a mysterious and awful combination of fruit juices and liquor," and had previously advocated for the country club favorite, the Southside, as an appropriate replacement. When the contest ran in May, over seventy-three entries vied for the prize: an engraved cup and two tickets to the Preakness. The only rules were that the drink had to be "tasty" and at least "tenuously" tied to the history and culture of Maryland. The judges were soon faced with ingredients ranging from ice cream to raw oysters and apricot brandy to crab seasoning.

Unfortunately for Kasper, his favorite entry, Andy Ervin's personal Southside recipe, was eliminated early on by fellow judge Joe Lombardo of WFBR radio, but soon the judges unanimously chose—to the extent of ordering another round—the Mr. Pim, submitted by Jack Raines, a Social Security worker from Glen Burnie. Like the Preakness cocktail that came before it, the Mr. Pim is a rather conservative entry and is really little more than a lengthened whiskey sour with rye whiskey as the base spirit. Raines did a pretty good job with theming too: "Mr." stood for "Maryland rye" and "Pim" was simply an abbreviation of Pimlico, although he would lose a few points from the judges for failing to realize that Maryland rye as no longer produced in-state. As far as taste was concerned, Kasper and the other judges remarked that it had a "nice lemon to override the solid rye body."

❦

## JACK RAINES'S MR. PIM

1½ ounce Maryland Straight Rye Whiskey (most likely Pikesville was used at the time)
1 tablespoon rich simple syrup (two parts sugar to water)
1 dash of bitters (presumably Angostura)
¼ lemon squeezed
club soda

Build in a lowball or old-fashioned glass. Squeeze in lemon wedge. Add cracked ice and top off with club soda. Stir and serve.

The victory of the Mr. Pim and Rob Kasper over the dreaded Black-Eyed Susan would be short-lived. At the time, John "Tommy" Manfuso Jr., one of the track owners who sat as a judge throughout the competition, stated that Pimlico was looking to change the Preakness drink for the 1988 race. An improved Susan was rolled out, but it was not one of the contest winners, on the grounds that they were "too complicated" for the staff to pre-mix before the event. A whiskey sour was too hard to pre-mix? This statement had us scratching our heads.

This new rendition of the Susan, supposedly chosen because it was light and durable, was described as better-looking and fruitier than the original, but it ultimately left Kasper and his judging panel less than impressed when they reunited for a round of them at the Harvey House.

—◦◦◦—

## 1988 "NEW SUSAN"

*Recipe adapted by Rob Kasper, the* Baltimore Sun

½ ounce vodka
½ ounce rum (light or dark was not specified)
½ ounce peach schnapps
6 ounces orange juice
1 ounces pink grapefruit juice
1 ounce pineapple juice

Shake with ice and serve in an ice-filled commemorative Preakness glass; if unavailable, use a highball or Collins.

So, can the Black-Eyed Susan be improved upon? At home, definitely. On the Pimlico infield, probably not. Cocktails batched in mass quantities always suffer in translation from their single-serve incarnations. Untold horrors are visited upon the venerable mint julep before it is served to the common folk at the Kentucky Derby—first, but not least being the use of the blended, dumbed-down version of Early Times Whiskey (that's right: it's not bourbon!). The Susan recipes old and new—a possible exception with the crème de menthe one—are not "bad" drinks, just a bit unimaginative. Should you make these at home for a Preakness party, you could always upgrade to fresh juice. For vodkas, don't use anything too pricey, though you could always strengthen the local ties by using either Sloop Betty from Blackwater or Maryland Blue Crab from Fiore.

# CHAPTER 18

# 1980s: THE ORANGE CRUSH

In Maryland, the arrival of beach weather means that Orange Crush season has arrived. Once again, the exact history of this drink is sketchy, but it is believed to have first appeared in Ocean City, Maryland, at the Harborside Bar & Grill sometime in the late 1980s. There is some controversy as to whether or not the Orange Crush really originated in Maryland, as Waterman's Surfside Grille in Virginia Beach also lays claim to have invented the drink. Regardless of who was first, it is the Maryland-style recipe that is predominantly served today, and even Waterman's reformulated its original recipe sometime in the early 2000s to bring it in line with prevailing tastes.

The standard recipe is an uncomplicated mix of orange juice, citrus-flavored vodka, orange liqueur of some kind and a splash of lemon-lime soda—usually Sprite—all served over crushed ice in a highball or pint glass. To be considered a proper Orange Crush, the orange juice must be fresh-squeezed from one whole orange, most of the time from a large, bar-mounted orange press.

Today, you can order an Orange Crush in almost any bar in the Baltimore metro area, and it is almost unavoidable during the summer charity party season in any area close to the water. While it is not and never claims to be the most complex drink ever to come out of the state of Maryland, the Orange Crush has definitely taken its place as one of those Baltimore novelties that your out-of-state friends have to order when they are in town visiting.

## ORANGE CRUSH

2 ounces Smirnoff Orange vodka
1 ounce triple sec
juice of one whole orange
splash of Sprite

Served in a pint glass, over crushed ice, with an orange slice.

## WHERE TO GET THE ORANGE CRUSH

HARBORSIDE BAR & GRILLE
12841 South Harbor Road
Ocean City, MD 21842
(410) 213-1846

MAMAS ON THE HALFSHELL
2901 O'Donnell Street
Baltimore, MD 21224
(410) 276-3160

RYLEIGHS OYSTER (MULTIPLE LOCATIONS)
Federal Hill
36 East Cross Street
Baltimore, MD 21230
(410) 539-2093 (main number)
www.ryleighs.com

Hunt Valley
22 Padonia Road
Hunt Valley, MD 21093

Mount Vernon
1225 Cathedral Street
Baltimore, MD 21201

# PART VII

—◈◈◈—

# THE COCKTAIL RENAISSANCE

## 1985–PRESENT

*In order to be a good bartender now, your drink has to tell a story.*
—*Perez Klebahn*

The 1990s marked a huge turning point in the cocktail industry. Both classic cocktail recipes and classic cocktail ingredients have undergone a major resurgence, but not just in an "everything old is new again" sort of way but also a renewed spirit of innovation in the field. New, culinary mixology endeavors existed alongside the speakeasy craze, and bartenders worldwide have regained the near rock star status they once had.

Keeping the historical trend, we here in Maryland, and Baltimore in particular, were lagging a bit behind the curve, but now we are surging back with a vengeance. The murmurs have been there since about 2010, but now our state's resident talents are up there serving world-class drinks but losing none of the quirky, hometown flair we have come to love. In this section, we come to the end of our narrative but certainly not the end of our story. Now we take a look at the present and get to "peak under the hood" of some of the fantastic drinks being served in our bars and restaurants this very moment. We may not have gotten to everyone, and yes, we have certainly missed someone's favorite bar or mixologist, but that's why we've named our website—and the subtitle to this book—"A History of Drinking" and not "*The* History of Drinking." These are the dangers of cocktail writing: it's highly personalized, sometimes heavily biased and often fraught with omissions, and maybe every once in a while, we get the facts completely wrong.

In closing, we'd like to give one final round of thanks to the bartenders and mixologists who have helped us along this journey and for providing the recipes that follow.

# CHAPTER 19

# MODERN COCKTAILS

## DOUG ATWELL

Rye
807 South Broadway
Baltimore, MD 21231
(443) 438-3296

⸎

## DIAMONDBACK NO. 5

2 ounces Pikesville rye whiskey
¾ ounce Laird's bonded apple brandy
¾ ounce yellow Chartreuse liqueur
Art in the Age's Root liqueur
sugar cube
lemon peel

Combine rye, brandy and Chartreuse in a mixing glass. Add ice
and stir. Rinse a chilled rocks glass with Root liqueur, discarding
excess. Place a sugar cube in the glass with a splash of water and
muddle. Strain in rye mixture and garnish with a large swath of
lemon peel.

—◦◦◦—

## VIKING DAISY

*"The name comes from the flowers used in the blanket placed around the Preakness winner's neck," Atwell said. "Viking daisies are used since Black-Eyed Susans are not yet in season."*

1½ ounces Edinburgh gin
¾ ounce strawberry syrup
¾ ounce freshly squeezed lemon juice
½ ounce yellow Chartreuse
1 dash Bar Keep fennel bitters

Shake with ice and strain into a chilled cocktail glass. Garnish with a lemon peel.

Strawberry syrup recipe:
In a heatproof container, pour 32 ounces 1:1 simple syrup (granulated sugar dissolved in boiling water) over 4 cups hulled and quartered fresh strawberries. Cover and let steep overnight. Strain and refrigerate. Syrup will last at least two weeks.

## BRENDAN DORR

B&O American Brasserie
Hotel Monaco Baltimore
2 North Charles Street
Baltimore, MD 21201

—◦◦◦—

## EL OSO

*Spanish for "The Bear," this cocktail was the winner of the 2010 US National Barenjager Cocktail Competition. Upon tasting, the judges called it "a perfectly balanced cocktail" and "an instant classic."*

1¾ ounce Partida Anejo Tequila
¾ ounce Bärenjäger
⅓ ounce Luxardo Maraschino Liqueur
2 dashes Bitter Truth Jerry Thomas Own Decanter Bitters
dehydrated orange wheel, for garnish

Combine all liquid ingredients in a mixing glass. Add ice and stir. Strain into a lowball glass with the dehydrated orange wheel on the bottom of the glass and two large ice cubes on top.

—◦◦◦—

## LINE STATE PUNCH

oleo-saccharum*
½ cup fresh lemon juice
2½ cups Pikesville Rye Whiskey
2½ cups yellow Chartreuse
2½ cups Laird's 7½ yr. Old Apple Brandy
4 cups the Tea Spot "Earl of Grey," infused with ginger**

Combine oleo-saccharum and lemon juice in a 1-gallon punch bowl. Stir to dissolve sugar and then add the remaining ingredients. Add large block ice to chill and grate nutmeg and cinnamon over the top. Serves 10–12 guests.

*Oleo-saccharum: Peel 8 lemons with a vegetable peeler, placing the peels in a mixing bowl. Add the sugar and muddle the contents for 2–3 minutes. Allow the mixture to sit for 1 hour, stirring and muddling occasionally. Cover and refrigerate until ready for use.

**"Earl of Grey" infused with ginger: Cold brew 4 heaping tablespoons of the Tea Spot "Earl of Grey" tea into 4 cups of cold water. Take 1 small inch-long piece of fresh ginger root and zest it into the mixture. Allow mixture to steep for 2 hours minimum. For a stronger and bitterer taste, allow mixture to steep longer.

# AARON JOSEPH

Wit & Wisdom
200 International Drive
Baltimore, MD 21202

—◦◦◦—

## COPPERHEAD

1½ ounces rye whisky
½ ounce orange juice
½ ounce lemon juice
¾ ounces pear gastrique
½ egg white

Place all ingredients in cocktail shaker without ice. Shake well. Add ice. Shake well. Double strain into cocktail coupe.

—◦◦◦—

## FARRAGUT COCKTAIL

1 ounce Four Roses bourbon
¼ ounce lemon juice
¼ ounce orange juice
¼ ounce maple sugar
2 dashes of Angostura bitters

In a cocktail shaker, mix bourbon, lemon and orange juice, maple sugar and bitters together. Shake vigorously.

Fill a double old fashioned glass with ice and strain into the glass. Garnish with cinnamon zest and orange peel.

—◦◦◦—

## PAPA NA PUA

1½ ounces hibiscus-infused Papa's Pilar Blonde Rum
1 ounce fresh grapefruit juice
½ ounce fresh lime juice
¾ ounce honey syrup

Place all ingredients in cocktail shaker with ice. Shake well. Strain into cocktail coupe. Garnish with lime peel and marigold flower.

—⟨⟩—

## PRESERVATION PUNCH

*This drink was Aaron's contribution to the "Rye Rocks at the Walters" gala in January 2015 to benefit the Walters Art Gallery. His innovative use of almond milk updates the traditional strained milk punch for this age of lactose-intolerance but is mighty tasty in its own right.*

*Serves 8 to 10 people*
7½ ounces of Copper Fox rye whisky
3 ounces lime juice
6 ounces of orange dulce tea
6 ounces spiced kumquat syrup
6 ounces almond milk

Combine the whisky, lime juice, tea and syrup into a large container and mix with a whisk. Heat up the almond milk to a slow boil and pour it into the premade mixture of punch. Let it sit for five minutes. After letting mixture rest pour it in a fine strainer or chinois strainer lined with a coffee filter. Allow time for mixture to completely strain through filter. After strained place in punch bowl and add a large piece of ice to chill punch. Once chilled garnish punch with apple slices and grated cinnamon and serve.

—⟨⟩—

## RECIPE FOR KUMQUAT SYRUP

1½ cups water
1½ teaspoons coriander
½ teaspoon black peppercorns
2 teaspoons cinnamon
1 vanilla bean
½ pound kumquats
3½ cups fresh pressed apple juice
2 cups sugar

Add water to a large cooking pot and place coriander, peppercorns, cinnamon sticks and vanilla bean into water. Heat on medium to low heat for 25 minutes. This allows the spices to steep and extract flavor for the syrup. After steeping introduce kumquats to mixture and allow to cook for ten minutes. After ten minutes introduce apple juice and sugar and heat till sugar is completely dissolved. It may help to stir to allow sugar to not settle on bottom and burn. Remove from pot and chill before mixing.

## JEFF LEVY

Sascha's 527
527 North Charles Street
Baltimore, MD 21201

—❦❦❦—

## THE JEFFERSON

⅔ ounce homemade simple syrup (1 part water to 1 parts sugar)
9 dashes Peychauds bitters
13 dashes orange bitters
1 ounce Luxardo Amaro Abano
2 ounces Templeton rye

The recipe is to be built in a glass filled with ice. Stir for fourteen to sixteen revolutions. Strain over flamed orange peel into a chilled rocks glass.

# CHAPTER 20

# ORPHANS AND MISCELLANY

Sometimes you simply can't find the origin story for a drink—after all, we are dealing with what David Wondrich refers to as "history agreed upon in a bar." The following drinks all have some tacit connection with either the state of Maryland or the city of Baltimore but either originated somewhere entirely different or their creation stories have vanished into the mists of time. They are included here simply for your enjoyment.

—⚬⚬⚬—

## BALTIMORE BANG

*This is a variation on a whiskey sour that adds apricot brandy or liqueur to the mix. The original version is served straight up in a chilled martini glass, but spirits columnist Jason Wilson prefers Derek Brown's version, served over ice. Adapted from Derek Brown, at the Passenger in Northwest Washington.*

1½ ounces bourbon
¾ ounce freshly squeezed lemon juice
½ ounce apricot brandy
¼ ounce simple syrup
twist of orange peel, for garnish

Fill a cocktail shaker halfway with ice. Add the bourbon, lemon juice, apricot brandy and simple syrup. Shake well, then strain into an ice-filled rocks or old-fashioned glass. Garnish with a twist of orange peel.

To make simple syrup, combine ½ cup of sugar and ½ cup of water in a small saucepan over medium heat, stirring until the sugar dissolves. Bring to a slow rolling boil, then reduce the heat to medium-low and cook for 5 minutes. Transfer to a heatproof container and let cool to room temperature.

## BALTIMORE BRACER

1 ounce brandy
1 ounce anisette
1 egg white

Shake all ingredients with ice, strain into a cocktail glass and serve.

## BALTIMORE ZOO

*Though apparently named after what is now the Maryland Zoo, this drink in fact originated at Purdue University sometime in the 1990s. One way to describe it is a glorified Long Island Iced Tea without the coke. Apparently, Harry's Chocolate Shop in West Lafayette, Indiana, serves the "best" Baltimore Zoos. Recipe adapted from drinksmixer.com.*

1 ounce vodka
1 ounce light rum
1 ounce gin
1 ounce triple sec
1 ounce Southern Comfort peach liqueur
1 ounce amaretto almond liqueur
1 ounce grenadine syrup
1 ounce sweet and sour mix
1 splash beer

Add the liquors and grenadine to a highball glass with ice. Top off with sweet and sour mix, add a splash of beer and stir.

———

# LORD BALTIMORE COCKTAIL

*From* Beverages de Luxe, *as served at the Pendennis Club, Louisville, Kentucky.*

Fill mixing glass with shaved ice, juice of one-half lime, one jigger Scotch whiskey and one-half jigger Red Curacao. Stir and strain in cocktail glass.

———

# MARYLAND SQUIRREL

*Part of Gary Regan's "squirrel sours" family of drinks, named for the nutty taste of the crème de noyau. It was dubbed "Maryland" for the presence of rye whiskey. Recipe adapted from* The Joy of Mixology *by Gary Regan.*

1½ ounces straight rye whiskey
¾ ounce crème de noyau
½ ounce fresh lemon juice
1 lemon twist for garnish

Shake and strain into a chilled cocktail glass. Add the garnish.

# SOURCES

## BOOKS

Albert, Bridget, and Mary Barranco. *Market-Fresh Mixology: Cocktails for Every Season.* Chicago: Surrey Books, 2008.

Andrews, Lewis R. *Maryland's Way: The Hammond-Harwood House Cook Book.* Annapolis, MD: Hammond-Harwood House Association, 1963.

Andrews, Matthew Page. *The Fountain Inn Diary.* New York: R.R. Smith, 1948.

Beirne, Francis F. *The Amiable Baltimoreans.* New York: Dutton, 1951.

Bomberger, Maude A. *Colonial Recipes, from Old Virginia and Maryland Manors, with Numerous Legends and Traditions Interwoven.* New York: Neale Publishing Company, 1907.

Buglass, Alan J. *Handbook of Alcoholic Beverages Technical, Analytical and Nutritional Aspects.* Chichester, West Sussex, England: John Wiley & Sons, 2011.

DeGroff, Dale, and George Erml. *The Craft of the Cocktail: Everything You Need to Know to Be a Master Bartender, with 500 Recipes.* New York: Clarkson Potter/Publishers, 2002.

Duffy, Patrick Gavin, and Robert Jay Misch. *The Official Mixer's Manual: The Standard Guide for Professional & Amateur Bartenders throughout the World.* Garden City, NY: Doubleday, 1975.

Franscell, Ron. *The Crime Buff's Guide to Outlaw Washington, DC.* Guilford, CT: Globe Pequot Press, 2012.

Ganim, Tony, and Mary Elizabeth Faulkner. *The Modern Mixologist: Contemporary Classic Cocktails.* Chicago: Surrey Books, 2010.

Helberg, Kristin. *The Belvedere and the Man Who Saved It.* Baltimore, MD: Pumpkin Publications, 1986.

Hess, Robert. *Essential Bartender's Guide: How to Create Truly Great Cocktails.* New York: Mud Puddle Books, 2008.

Howard, Jane Grant Gilmore. *Fifty Years in a Maryland Kitchen.* Baltimore, MD: Turnbull Bros., 1873.

Regan, Gary. *The Joy of Mixology.* New York: Clarkson Potter, 2003.

Simmons, Marcia, and Jonas Halpren. *DIY Cocktails: A Simple Guide to Creating Your Own Signature Drinks.* Avon, MA: Adams Media, 2011.

Steers, Edward. *Blood on the Moon: The Assassination of Abraham Lincoln.* Lexington: University Press of Kentucky, 2001.

Stieff, Frederick Philip. *Eat, Drink & Be Merry in Maryland: An Anthology from a Great Tradition.* New York: G.P. Putnam's Sons, 1932.

Straub, Jacques. *Straub's Manual of Mixed Drinks.* Chicago: R.F. Welsh, 1913.

Washburne, George R., and Stanley Bronner. *Beverages de Luxe.* 2nd ed. Louisville, KY: Wine and Spirit Bulletin, 1914.

Wondrich, David. *Imbibe!: From Absinthe Cocktail to Whiskey Smash, a Salute in Stories and Drinks to "Professor" Jerry Thomas, Pioneer of the American Bar.* New York: Perigee Book/Penguin Group, 2007.

———. *Punch: The Delights (and Dangers) of the Flowing Bowl: An Anecdotal History of the Original Monarch of Mixed Drinks, with More than Forty Historic Recipes, Fully Annotated, and a Complete Course in the Lost Art of Compounding Punch*. New York: Penguin Group, 2010.

Writers' Program of the Works Progress Administration. *Maryland, a Guide to the Old Line State*. New York: Oxford University Press, 1941.

## NEWSPAPERS AND PERIODICALS

*Baltimore Sun*. "Admiral Keleher Funeral Today." July 25, 1962.

———. "Apple Toddy A Year Old." January 2, 1900.

———. "As It Used To Be." December 26, 1888.

———. "A Crisp New Year." January 3, 1899.

———. "Eastern Sho' Apple Toddy." December 23, 1906.

———. "Fashions In Drinks." December 25, 1901.

———. "4,000 Dance Night Away at Second Preakness Ball." May 16, 1937.

———. "Gay Thousands Dance in Honor of Preakness." May 16, 1936.

———. "Lithuanians Are Focus of 'Showcase.'" May 23, 1976.

———. "Marylanders at the Front." Special dispatch, April 27, 1897.

———. "Odd Stories of Baltimore Town." October 10, 1909.

———. "Old Garden Holds Tales of Romance and War." September 27, 1925.

———. "Preakness Cocktail Picked by Supreme Court of Five." April 29, 1936.

————. "What of Prize London Drink? Here, Barman Says, Try Mine." January 26, 1948.

Blumberg, Jess. "Southside Wars." *Baltimore Magazine*, June 1, 2010.

Bready, James H. "Maryland Rye: A Whiskey the Nation Long Fancied—But Now Has Let Vanish." *Maryland Historical Magazine* 85, no. 4 (Winter 1990).

Connolly, James P. "War between the Tastes." *Baltimore Sun*, July 13, 1947.

Frances, Yearley Hiss. "Society—New Year's Day to be Marked in Proper Fashion." *Baltimore Sun*, December 31, 1933.

Henry, H. "Beer Soup, Bread with Almost." *Baltimore Sun*, December 12, 1971.

Kasper, Rob. "And the Winner Is." *Baltimore Sun*, May 13, 1987.

————. "A Contest for the Preakness." *Baltimore Sun*, April 5, 1987.

————. "A Preakness Loser." *Baltimore Sun*, May 14, 1986.

Kenney, Sarah Lynn. "Maryland's Alcohol Culture: Topographic and Economic Influences on the Social Drinking Culture of the Colonial Chesapeake." *History Matters* (May 2009): 43.

"Kosher Boh." Citypaper.com. September 21, 2011. http://www.citypaper. com/bob/2011/bcp-cms-1-1205854-migrated-story-cp-20110921-bobni-20110921,0,6870357.story#sthash.l1CVU8pl.dpuf.

L.C.A. "Christmas Echoes, with the Story of the Forgotten Recipe for an Insidious Drink." *Baltimore Sun*, December 27, 1911.

Mayhugh, Jess. "Cocktail Confidential: The Handcrafted Mixed Drink Is Making a Comeback in Baltimore." *Baltimore Magazine*, September 2013.

Meacham, Sarah Hand. "'They Will Be Adjudged by Their Drink, What Kinde of Housewives They Are': Gender, Technology, and Household Cidering in England and the Chesapeake, 1690 to 1760." *Virginia Magazine of History and Biography* 111, no. 2 (2003): 117–50.

Price, G. Jefferson, III. "An Ode to the City's Premier Mixologists." *Baltimore Sun*, July 14, 2002. http://articles.baltimoresun.com/2002-07-14/topic/0207130306_1_watering-hole-calvert-house-bartender.

Washington Post. "Baltimore, Wrapped in Mystery." January 18, 2004. http://www.washingtonpost.com/wp-dyn/content/article/2004/01/18/AR2005033107125_2.html.

White, Emmet H. "The Cocktail Party in Baltimore: A History." *Baltimore Sun*, September 25, 1971.

# WEBSITES

"Arthur McGinnis and the Great Whiskey Heist." Those Pre-Pro Whiskey Men! http://pre-prowhiskeymen.blogspot.com/2011/08/arthur-mcginnis-and-great-whiskey-heist_25.html.

"Baltimore's Tiki History." Johnny Dollar's Vault. http://jjohnnydollar.blogspot.com/2007/04/baltimore-tiki-history-hawaiian-room-in.html.

Brown, Alton. "Alton Brown on the History of Eggnog." Mental Floss. http://mentalfloss.com/article/31813/alton-brown-history-eggnog.

Clarke, Paul. "The Diamondback." Cocktail Chronicles, April 27, 2009. http://www.cocktailchronicles.com/2009/04/27/3030-11-the-diamondback.

"Decade by Decade." The Chanticleer Society. http://chanticleersociety.org/wikis/timeline/decade-by-decade.aspx.

"Diamondback Lounge." NYPL Digital Collections. http://digitalcollections.nypl.org/items/b0d65bdd-78b9-7d0a-e040-e00a18065084.

"Diamondback No.5." Garden & Gun, February 1, 2014. http://gardenandgun.com/article/diamondback-no5.

Dietsch, Michael. "A Guide to Defunct Cocktail Ingredients." Serious Eats, September 12, 2013. http://drinks.seriouseats.com/2013/09/guide-to-defunct-cocktail-ingredients-bitters-liqueurs-cordials-abbots-bokers-caperitif-out-of-production.html.

Drummond, Ned. "The Drink of My Forefathers: Virytas." Stuff I Make—Maneating Flower's Blog, November 27, 2010. http://maneatingflower.blogspot.com/2010/11/drink-of-my-forefathers-virytas.html.

Eaton, Lorraine. "Oceanfront Restaurant's 'Crush' Drink Creates Viral Buzz." *Virginian-Pilot*, August 14, 2012. http://hamptonroads.com/2012/08/oceanfront-restaurants-crush-drink-creates-viral-buzz.

"Hawaiian Room, Baltimore, MD (restaurant)—Tiki Central." Tiki Central, July 30, 2011. http://www.tikiroom.com/tikicentral/bb/viewtopic.php?topic=40757&forum=2.

Putney, Stewart. "Weekly Cocktail #35: The Diamondback." Putney Farm. http://putneyfarm.com/2012/11/02/weekly-cocktail-35-the-diamondback.

Regan, Gary. "El Oso." Gazregan. http://www.gazregan.com/2012/05/101-best-new-cocktails/el-oso.

Saucier, Ted. "Bottoms Up." The Daily Details. http://www.details.com/blogs/daily-details/2008/09/bottoms-up-by-ted-saucier.html.

York, Bill. "Chesapeake Bay Bitters." The Bitter End Bitters. http://www.bitterendbitters.com/index.php.

# INDEX

# ABOUT THE AUTHORS

Lifelong Marylanders, Gregory and Nicole are the "alcohologists" behind A History of Drinking, the cocktail blog that pairs random and often obscure historical events with appropriate cocktails. Active in the national and online cocktail communities since 2009, they have created custom cocktails for Hiram Walker, Crown Royal and many other brands. When they aren't immersed in the spirit world, Gregory is an instructional designer for Harford Community College and Nicole works in finance. This is their first book.